# Feminism and
# Islamic Fundamentalism

**Haideh Moghissi** is an associate professor of sociology and women's studies at Atkinson College, York University, Toronto. Before leaving Iran in 1984, she was a senior archivist in the Iran National Archives. She was a founder of the National Union of Women and member of its first executive board and the editorial board of *Barabari* (Equality) and *Zanan Dar Mobarezeh* (Women in Struggle).

# Feminism and Islamic Fundamentalism

## The Limits of Postmodern Analysis

HAIDEH MOGHISSI

ZED BOOKS
London & New York

*Feminism and Islamic Fundamentalism* was first published by
Zed Books Ltd, 7 Cynthia Street, London N1 9JF, UK,
and Room 400, 175 Fifth Avenue, New York, NY 10010, USA in 1999

Distributed in the USA exclusively by Palgrave, a division of LLC,
St Martin's Press, 175 Fifth Avenue, New York, NY 10010

Second impression, 2002

Typeset in Joanna by Lucy Morton & Robin Gable, Grosmont
Cover designed by Andrew Corbett
Printed and bound in the United Kingdom
by Biddles Ltd, *www.biddles.co.uk*

A catalogue record for this book is available from the British Library

**Library of Congress Cataloging-in-Publication Data**
Moghissi, Haideh, 1944–
    Feminism and Islamic fundamentalism / Haideh Moghissi
        p.  cm.
    Includes bibliographical references and index.
    ISBN 1–85649–589–2 (hb). — ISBN 1–85649–590–6 (pbk)
    1. Muslim women.   2. Islamic fundamentalism.   3. Women—Legal
suits, laws, etc. (Islamic law)   4. Feminism—Religious aspects—
Islam.   5. Women—Islamic countries—Social conditions.   I. Title.
HQ1170.M64   1999                                       99–22771
305.48´6971—dc21                                           CIP

ISBN 1 85649 589 2 (Hb)
ISBN 1 85649 590 6 (Pb)

# Contents

# Preface

The idea of writing a book about feminism and Islamic fundamentalism developed out of the discomfort I felt over several years as I watched and listened to academic debates on the subject. Gradually, one noticed a shift in accounts about women's lives in Islamic societies, from a sympathetic appreciation of the plight of women under fundamentalist rule to extravagant affirmations of Muslim women's 'agency', gender-awareness, empowerment and security within a protected space. In an heroic effort to rescue 'Islam' from its bad reputation in the treatment of women, discussions blurred distinctions between 'Islam' as a faith, 'Islam' as the ideology of a movement in opposition, and Islam as a ruling system, that is, Islamic fundamentalism.

As if charmed by a drumbeat from afar, some scholars have even yielded to the Islamists' intellectual seductions, transforming the robust defence of Islamic faith and the urgent need to protect Muslim minorities in the West into an apology for fundamentalist practice where it needs no defence, and where, in fact, it exercises a terrible monopoly of political and cultural power. In this they confuse the principle of recognizing and affirming the rights of Muslim minorities in the West with an unprincipled tolerance for the oppressive political and cultural practices in countries where Muslims form a majority and the full power of government is in the hands of a theocratic elite. In the name of anti-imperialism these intellectuals turn a blind eye to the consequences of such utopian experiments for people actually living under fundamentalist rule; and little by little, these discursive slippages and confusions and outright abandonments have cost much to the region's women (and men), as they struggle for a more humane and democratic system, a quality of intellectual freedom taken for granted in the West.

These apologetic accounts were more troubling because they were not simply journalistic reports which combined rudimentary observations and government propaganda with exotic fantasies and the reflections of taxi-drivers who drive the reporters around in Tehran, Cairo or other Middle Eastern cities. What has disturbed me the most – and, I know that, in this, I am not alone – have been the arguments elegantly presented by secular Middle East scholars, including some feminists of prominence.

This book is an attempt to illuminate the contradictory implications of academic theorization for those theorized. I am aware that in this I may have amplified, unwittingly, the political impact of the postmodern, post-colonial perspectives. The scholars whose views I have opposed can at least take comfort in finding that their academic works have some real and earnest connection with the 'outside' world and with the realm of politics, inspiring debate and contestation. Is this not what we, as academics, appreciate and aspire to?

The remarkable struggle of women throughout the Middle East for democratization of their culture and society, including the struggles of Iranian women, to whom I am politically, intellectually and emotionally closely associated, have provided me with a never-ending source of inspiration and strength. I bow to their resilience, intelligence and ingenuity and owe them a great debt of gratitude. I hope this book makes a modest contribution to debates and struggles for political democracy, for human rights and social and cultural change in Islamic societies.

I am grateful to others for more particular reasons. I thank Atkinson College, York University, for the support provided by two Research Grants. I would like to thank Louise Murray at Zed Books for her confidence in this book since its inception and for her support throughout the process. I also thank Justin Dyer for his careful copy-editing and good suggestions. Thanks are also due to Ali Rahnema for his friendship and support. I am deeply grateful to

Mark Goodman for many stimulating discussions and helpful critiques, and for his generous editorial contributions. I thank Shahrzad Mojab, with whom I have shared and discussed many of the intellectual and political ideas in this book. Special thanks are due to Saeed Rahnema for his unfailing support and for always being the most critical and, often, least forgiving reader of my writings. His critiques and constructive suggestions helped me to improve the manuscript. It should go without saying that the short-comings are all mine.

# Introduction

Islamic societies appear to be caught in the grip of two contradictory social currents. As Islamic metaphors, symbols and prescriptions become forms of political expression, more people throughout the Middle East look to Islam as a liberatory project and conformity to the sacred texts, a revitalized *Shari'a*, and the rule of Muslim jurists appeal to the disenfranchised masses as the only hope for meaningful change in their lives. At the same time, in countries where Islamists have taken power, the number grows of those who, disillusioned by the Islamists' failed promises, are turning their backs on Islamic militancy. Islam's legitimacy fades as the gap widens between rich and poor, as the professional middle class finds its position increasingly precarious and autocratic Muslim rulers become more evidently corrupt. Claims to construct a just society prove themselves farcical and, except in their determination to curtail women's rights, fundamentalist regimes are seen to do no more than preserve the status quo, only putting a *Shari'a* hat (*kolah-e Sharii*) on it.[1] Far from constructing a just society, Muslim rulers are understood to be continuing economic and political policies which, in the mid-1970s, led to the crisis that gave rise to the fundamentalist movements. Cultural repression and moral crusades targeting women and youth provoke disaffection. But through the manipulation of people's needs and a cynical use of intimidation and terror, the Islamists secure their power, presenting a formidable challenge to secular liberal nationalist and socialist projects throughout the Middle East and North Africa.

Women lose much more than men as a result of the social conservatism that is everywhere the marker of fundamentalist movements. From Afghanistan to Algeria to Sudan, Pakistan and Iran – indeed, everywhere in the Islamic societies – women are systematically brutalized and caught in a deadly crossfire between the secular and fundamentalist forces.

Under the iron fist of the Taliban, day-to-day life for the people of Afghanistan is a nightmarish experience – an inevitable result of a devastating war in one of the world's poorest countries. Today, Afghanistan bears the brunt of foreign occupation, arising out of the rivalry between the former Soviet Union and the United States. The war of 1979–89 against the Soviets left this country of fifteen million with one million dead and eight million uprooted – not to mention an enormous number of wounded and maimed. But the Taliban only provides the latest version of authoritarian rule in Afghanistan. Even if one could find the Taliban's bizarre methods dreadfully funny – ordering men to grow beards, banning soccer and music and wearing white shoes (white is the official colour for the Taliban), the noonday roundup of men for prayers – the persecution of women under various versions of Islamic fundamentalism, be it the former rulers of 'liberated' Afghanistan, the Mujahedin or the Taliban, is nothing but wretchedly tragic.[2] Women have suffered terribly since the outbreak of civil strife in Afghanistan.[3] Under Borhan-ul-Din Rabbani's Mujahedin-led government they became, officially, second-class subjects. Under the Taliban, the situation has deteriorated yet further. In effect, women are kept under house arrest. They are banned from attending schools. They cannot work outside the home. They cannot leave their homes, except in the company of a male relative.

In Sudan, the establishment of strict, Shari'a-based rule by the Islamic National Front (NIF) also weighs heavily on a population which, like the rest of the Middle Eastern and North African societies (excepting Saudi Arabia), had lived before under a less rigid code of 'popular' Islam.[4] The Islamization policy in Sudan extends to non-Arab and non-Muslim minorities. The Sudanese government's 'ethnic cleansing' includes abduction, systemic rape, murder, slavery and deliberately caused famine.[5]

Since 1992, Algerian women, too, have had to bear a heavy dose of the fundamentalists' bitter medicine. The civilian population is caught between forces of the Armed Islamic Group (AIG) and the military government. But as an Algerian journalist reports, 'fundamentalists are hunting women' in particular (cited in Bennoune, 1995: 185).[6] Women bear the full burden of the terror. Teenage girls and young women are routinely abducted, raped, burned and murdered. Among the many thousands of rape victims, some give birth after their rescue but prefer to go into hiding, rather than returning to their villages. The plight of these women is on the agenda of such organizations as the National Association for the Support of Children in Difficulties, who are pushing the government to remove, at least, the ban on abortion.[7]

Many of these terrors are known to the international community. So are the hypocritical policies of Western governments, such as Reagan's Iran–Contra affair and the arms sale to Iran's Ayatollah Khomeini, whose regime US officials condemned for its violations of human rights. Today, French President Jacques Chirac criticizes the 'barbaric excesses' of religious fanatics in opposition in Algeria[8] while his government maintains intimate ties with religious fanatics in Sudan, providing them with technical and military assistance including intelligence on opposition forces such as the Sudan People's Liberation Army (SPLA) (Connell, 1997: 36). Also well known is the financial and military aid provided to the Afghan Mujahedin by the US government and CIA during the civil war in Afghanistan; now, the USA supports the Taliban. The United States hopes that the Taliban's firm grip will allow the Turkmenistan gas pipeline to reach Pakistan via Western Afghanistan, bypassing Iran (Roy, 1997: 37–40).

Given the massive interests of the United States and other great powers in the Middle East and North Africa which underscores the militarization of the client states, favouring reliable allies and punishing non-collaborators, it would be foolish to hope that the policies of Western governments in the region will ever be guided by anything but greed and geostrategic priorities. To be sure, the treatment of women by fundamentalist regimes draws much attention in the West. Women loom large in scholarly and journalistic commentaries; and women's rights issues are identified in official statements and government reports. The issue, however, is often used ideologically to isolate and contain adversaries of great powers. It is never raised in connection with the region's oil-producing collaborators in the Arabian Peninsula.

In this context, appeals to those in Washington and elsewhere to respond coherently to Islamic regimes' human rights violations seem gravely naïve. At the same time, given the recurrent Islamophobia of media and governments in the West and the growing arsenal of racist imagery about Islam and Muslim women, targeting diasporic communities, writing critically about Islamic gendered practices and the devastating impact on women of Islamic fundamentalism forces upon one a great deal of personal and political anguish and self-doubt. The question is always whose interests are being served, and whose side one is taking. It is in this climate, perhaps, that certain scholars deny the more punishing features of Islamic practices and traditions, emphasizing, instead, the positive aspects of Islamic culture. Such a position, however, is highly problematic.

The best way to express solidarity with the Muslim diaspora is not to keep silent about oppressive features of one's own cultural tradition or the inhumane practices of fundamentalist regimes. One must maintain a clear focus and target. This means not participating in the destructive defensiveness which has shaped anti-colonial imagination in Islamic societies – to refuse self-glorification and self-pity. Pointing fingers at others assists the region's reactionary religious and political establishments in walling themselves off against internal challenges and popular demands. In the context of demoniz-ation of Islam and Muslims which we find in the West it is essential to defend the rights of Muslim communities to cultural autonomy and unhindered religious practices. The problem is that such a defence often involves what Deniz Kandiyoti describes as 'trans-posing' debates such as multiculturalism and identity politics situ-ated in the West to a different context (Kandiyoti, 1995: 28–9). To draw parallels between Muslim minorities in the West, where they do not hold state power to impose their views and their moral standards on others, and the Islamic movements and regimes in the Middle East and North Africa, where they do, is to confuse our-selves about who the real victims are. Consider, for example, *Hejab* (veiling) and debates in the West concerning its role in 'empowering' Muslim women by providing them a protected space. Under the rule of fundamentalists in the Middle East and North Africa, women who are persecuted, jailed and whipped for their non-compliance with *hejab* find the dress code anything but empowering. One can appreciate why the individuals who express such ideas do not live in the region.

Neither is it a sound argument that to take a critical stance against Muslim gendered practices in the Middle East may place us on the same side as the US State Department and other Western governments. In fact, nothing brings one as close to the foreign policy of Western powers as a 'hands off' approach. 'Cultural sensitivity' and 'cultural tolerance' provide an excuse to Western governments to conveniently put to bed their much-advertised concerns about women's rights, lack of democracy and freedom of expression in Islamic societies and to normalize trade relations. At no time has this fact been as clear as it is today. If the treatment of women in Iran, Afghanistan and Sudan is contrary to all internationally recognized (and signed) conventions, it is because *their* cultural beliefs, practices and ways of doing things are *different*; 'they' have *their* ways, 'we' have *ours*. We should be 'more accepting' of practices which are unacceptable *here* but admissible *there*. Hence, the continued massive arms sales and uninterrupted flow of trade.

Talking out of context about 'Muslim' cultural practices also obscures the profound heterogeneity of peoples from Muslim societies within or without the Middle East. People who live under Islamic laws are not bound together by a metaculture, even less by Islamist politics. Many are discriminated against and many more are severely punished for that reason alone. Which is to say 'difference' is not a term to use only for drawing attention to dissimilarities between 'Muslim' and 'Western' ways and views. It is also a useful term to note the contrast among the ways and views of people from 'Muslim' societies.

In writing about Islamic traditions and fundamentalist practices from a critical perspective, one takes a stand against both the Orientalist and Islamist streams of study. Both these perspectives obscure the complex web of class, gender, ethnic, religious and regional differences which separate rather than unite the ways of life, and particularly the political and ideological perspectives, of people in the Middle East. Critical writings challenge the typical Orientalist and fundamentalist identification of people in Islamic societies as Muslim conformists. Consider, for example, the declarations of Arab and Iranian intellectuals, including the petition of 127 Iranian intellectuals in exile, which were made against Ayatollah Khomeini's *fatwa* on Salman Rushdie. This was done at a time when many other Middle Eastern and Western scholars were coyly supporting the *fatwa*, using 'different cultural standards' as an excuse.

The point is that the political options for the Middle Eastern intellectual are not as narrow as is often implied. We are not forced to choose between passively keeping silent and minimizing the consequences of Islamic fundamentalism or siding with the bullying policy of foreign powers, particularly the United States, with its wanton bombing of Sudan and Afghanistan and its continuing assaults on Iraq. We can be against both. Opposing foreign intervention in Islamic societies does not require one to obscure the actual conditions of women's lives under Islamic rule or to soften the coercive power of Islamic movements and regimes.

In this book I have tried to explore and critique the intellectual tendencies which might be understood as making concessions to fundamentalist regimes and movements – in effect abandoning women to their iron rule. As Beth Baron remarks, the treatment of women provides compelling evidence of the repressive character of fundamentalist social and political practices, yet the subject is usually neglected in academic analysis (Baron 1996: 124). Is this tendency driven by fear of physical violence or by a paralysing anxiety lest one be accused of cultural insensitivity or 'Orientalist' tendencies? Or is it a postmodern specimen of the attitude to 'exotic' practices and institutions which, viewed from afar, are celebrated as 'authentic', 'local' responses to indigenous problems – and excused as inevitable because they 'fit' with the culture? Whatever the reason, despite their seemingly radical appearance I argue that such perspectives are quite conservative. Time and time again we have seen the sensitivity of authoritarian regimes to international pressure. The very least the international intellectual community can do is to not ease the pressure on Islamic fundamentalist regimes and movements in the name of respecting cultural difference and cultural authenticity.

As I discuss in Chapter 1, there is merit to the argument that there are more sides to women's experiences in Islamic societies than the horrors of life under fundamentalist regimes. No doubt, a one-sided analysis would conceal the spirit and the humanity of Muslim women and their strength and resilience in coping, as well as their long history of struggle for change. Besides, Islam varies in the restrictions it imposes on women. The level of rigidity implicated by the Islamic Shari'a depends on the level of society's socio-economic development and local cultural traditions. However, Qur'anic injunctions and Shari'a rulings, as interpreted by the local ulama (jurists), continue to define women's legal status and provide a basis for gendered social and cultural practices. It is a question of balance. For centuries women's sexuality and moral conduct has preoccupied Muslim men; men's needs and scripts have circumscribed women's lives and the extent of their participation in public affairs. The rise of Islamic fundamentalism in contemporary Middle Eastern and North African societies has accentuated this preoccupation and translated it into legal practices and bureaucratic rules.

In Chapter 2 I argue that the 'Muslim woman' who emerges in some academic writings which challenge negative imagery can be as one-sided and illusory as traditional accounts. For in the new understanding also Islam appears as an all-encompassing entity defining all that there is in the Middle East, with the difference that the 'Muslim woman' is presented as a wholly dignified, spiritually empowered being. Non-Westoxicated, she enjoys a balanced dose of public activity and moral restraint, an enviable security from the violence afflicting women in the developed West. If, in the Orientalist version, Islam is condemned for its unreformed and unreformable gender-oppressive character, in this neo-Orientalist version, it is applauded for its woman-friendly adaptability, its liberatory potential. It is quite justified to affirm women's experience and let women speak for themselves. But should this be done by refraining from a direct challenge to Islamic fundamentalism? Why is there so little outrage in the academic literature against the crimes targeting women in the name of religion? By not talking about the hardship of

women's life under fundamentalist rule, have not secular intellectuals accepted the limits imposed by Islamists, reducing opposition to
the level of abstraction?

I suggest in Chapters 3 and 4 that the debates on the 'Muslim
woman' have been strongly influenced by the vagaries of academic
fashion, particularly in North America, including postmodern
relativism, anti-Orientalism and identity politics. Outlining the core
arguments of postmodern relativism and Islamic fundamentalism, I
try to demonstrate that, ironically, the two share a common ground
– an unremitting hostility to the social, cultural and political processes
of change, originated in the West, known as modernity. Among
other similarities between postmodernists and fundamentalists are
their rejection of the West's project for the reforms of gender relations;
their enthusiastic appreciation of everything non-Western, and their
semi-critique of capitalism – neither rejecting capitalism altogether
nor envisioning a socialist society as a viable alternative.

I propose that anti-Orientalism and postmodernism may have
opened new possibilities for cultural inquiry, but in their rush to
give voice to those constructed as Other, they have entrapped themselves in the headlong pursuit of the 'exotic' and 'native'. If the
Orientalists created an illusory, shimmering image of Oriental Muslim
women, postmodernists confront them by turning the genre on its
head. In the process of validating 'Muslim women's' experience, the
harsh edges of fundamentalism are softened; and the image that
fundamentalists transmit of Muslim women as emblematic of cultural revival, integrity and authenticity is validated. In the end, the
postmodern relativists collude with the fundamentalists' culturalist
solutions to crises of modernity and of modernization.

Central to my arguments in Chapter 5 are two points. First, the
exploitative, uneven and discriminatory nature of development
associated with modernity in the West is an undeniable fact. But this
does not prove that premodern formations were better for women.
Neither can it persuade us to find irrelevant to the experience of
women in Islamic societies the rights that women have achieved in
the West. Second, feminism takes different forms and puts forth
different demands given differing social, economic and cultural
contexts. Different priorities, however, do not mean different aspir-

ations altogether. The women throughout the Middle East and North Africa who are challenging Islamization policies and who are struggling against the fundamentalists' 'culturally specific' roles and moral conduct aspire to – and are entitled to – the same basic rights that women enjoy in the West. To advise Middle Eastern women that they should look for women's rights to culturally authentic, home-grown ideologies, that is, the Islamic framework, is to argue that feminism is and must remain the privileged domain of women in the West. Such arguments also validate the fundamentalist teaching which singles out feminism and its Western values as the main enemy of women in Islamic societies.

Chapter 6 deals with gender politics of fundamentalists, once they take over the state power, using the most important case of Iran. To understand the gender politics of the Islamists since the 1979 Revolution (their crude Islamization practices in the early years; their masterful manipulation of feminist demands and feminist tactics in the years that followed) and the ebbs and flows of women's responses requires an analysis which takes into account the social and economic context in which the fundamentalists operate. A discussion of Islamization policies in Iran and women's responses to them seeks to warn against analyses which speak only of how well women cope, how remarkably they manoeuvre and how skilfully they try to preserve their humanity. Such analyses neglect the negative consequence of Islamic fundamentalism for women, religious minorities and non-dominant ethnic groups, secular nationalists and socialist intellectuals. For close to two decades, women's resistance has been expressed in many ingenuous forms, all rejecting the fundamentalist project and the Islamic orthodoxy it represents. Given this great variety of response, I ask, why is it that we hear only and echo the voices of Muslim female elites for whom Islam is the final solution and which alone, in their view, provides the path to women's emancipation?

The final chapter explores the possibilities and limits of Islamic feminism. Can Islam present 'a new revolutionary paradigm' and an alternative to 'Western feminism'? The question here is not one of compatibility between Islam and feminism. Feminism is diversified and flexible enough to embrace all individuals and movements which are self-identified or are identified by others as feminist based on distinguishable ideological and political characteristics. The problem arises, rather, with the attempt to push Islam on feminists in Islamic societies as the only 'culturally suitable' or workable project. In this way, women in Islamic societies are once more reduced to their 'Islamic' identity, erasing significant differences across regional, ethnic, religious, class and cultural lines.

The striking history of women's movements in several Middle Eastern societies and the existence of a remarkable feminist tradition in the region are evidenced by the voices of gender-conscious women who, since the nineteenth century, have articulated women's concerns in Islamic societies. Although many of these pioneers felt compelled to challenge the Islamic *Shari'a* and its misogynist instructions by resorting to more women-friendly Qur'anic interpretations, none carried their struggle under the banner of 'Islamic feminism'. In the push for 'Islamic feminism' we see the political and discursive influence of Islamic fundamentalism, as supporters of this line invade the agenda of secular intellectuals, including feminists. In truth, the 'exuberant' accounts of Islamic feminism reflect a profound defeatism which presumes the end of secular nationalist liberal and socialist projects in Islamic societies.

The complex dynamics of gender struggle in Islamic societies require much analytical focus. We need to reconsider old dogmas, ideological perceptions and cultural stereotypes, while validating the experiences and voices of women. No political event in the Middle East in the last two decades forces us to conclude that the region's solution for women (and men) is an Islamic one. Islamic fundamentalism does not provide an answer to the far reach of the West's economic, political and cultural domination in the Middle East, nor does it represent a 'culturally specific' alternative to 'modernism' as exercised under European and North American tutelage.

Having said all this, I am quite confident about the future of women's struggle for their legal rights and for democratization of cultures and societies in the Middle East. What prompts optimism is that habits developed out of even a partially completed break with secular modernity are hard to put on hold; reforms, although precarious, remain on the agenda. The reverse is also true. The more unreformed or more unevenly developed and more traditional a society, the more fundamentalists can speedily put into practice the backward, religiously conformist notions which they preach. This applies particularly to those notions which punish women. In the last two decades, women have spared no effort to win back, inch by inch, the grounds which they lost through 're-Islamization' policies in Iran, Sudan and Pakistan. These women are reclaiming their humanity, fighting to change structures and relations of gender power. The circumstance of women in Islamic cultures must be understood dialectically, as their determined resistance strains against forces of social, economic and political retardation.

## Notes

1. *Shari'a hat* (*kolah-e Sharii*) is an expression used to refer to the manipulation of Islamic rules for legitimizing an illegitimate action.

2. See *The Globe and Mail*, 7 December 1996.

3. Women were abducted and raped, their breasts cut off by their Muslim 'brothers', fighting against the Soviet forces. In refugee camps in Pakistan and Iran the religious and political rulers, capitulating to Pakistani and Iranian authorities, imposed strict 'Islamic' codes of seclusion and the veil, depriving women refugees without a male relative of receiving food, medical attention and education, turning women into baby machines in Muslim men's jihad (holy war) against the infidels (Wali, 1995: 176–7).

4. Fundamentalists' gender politics in Sudan follow the familiar pattern. Sexual segregation in public places and the imposition of a dress code symbolize Muslim cultural authenticity. The Law of Public Order controls women's movements and their moral behaviour through such practices as segregation of means of public transport and prohibition of dancing and partying. A woman must not be seen in a single man's house. Enacted in 1991, the Law of Personal Affairs (family law), sets the legal marriage age at ten for girls, legitimizes polygamy and declares man's unilateral right to divorce. (Report of the Omdrum Centre for Women's Studies, Cairo, Egypt, October 1998.)

5. The Nuba people suffer from what relief workers and African rights groups have identified as a genocide carried out by the NIF and its military wing. Preposterous hardships are imposed on women and children in the so-called 'peace camps.' See (Hale 1997: 47). See also *Guardian Weekly*, 25 August 1996, and *The Globe and Mail*, 21 October 1995.

6. For the AIG, all Algerians who are not on their side are infidels and deserve to die. The government, in its turn, uses everything in its power,

including terrorism, to stay in control; security forces have been implicated in several massacres attributed to the AIG. See *Guardian Weekly*, 2 February 1997.

7. See *International Herald Tribune*, 30 December 1997.
8. *Guardian Weekly*, 11 August 1996.

# Chapter 1

# Oriental Sexuality: Imagined and Real

The imagery of Islam as a peculiar religion, predisposed to maltreat the female sex, seems always to have existed. No other religion has so shamelessly been the target of demonization for its gender practices and no religion has so passionately and boldly barricaded itself against outside pressures. Gendered cultural practices and legal traditions are a recurring theme in travellers' tales, diplomats' reports and in the diaries of traders, physicians, teachers and other Europeans recruited by various Middle Eastern states – indeed whoever came in contact with Islamic societies. But it is particularly after the colonial encounter that we catch sight in European literary and scholarly works of the West's inferiorizing gaze. In colonial records, commentaries and descriptions of 'local' traditions report on cultural practices hostile to women, contemplating sanctimoniously how and when Muslim women can be liberated from the yoke of Muslim men. These stereotypes are often fraught with the sexual fantasies of the European male.

## Muslim Women Imagined

The relentless, dominating mentality behind the slanderous accounts and images of Muslims and Islamic lands is revealed in David Stannard's examination of the European mindset and of the sexual obsessions and inhibitions of the average European male prior to and at the time of Europe's adventures beyond its borders.

Unrestricted sex and unrestrained sexuality, Stannard argues, were among the sins projected upon non-European man. Indeed, whatever escaped Christian norms was seen as not only alien and foreign, but also overtly sexual and beastly, primitive, lustful, ungodly. In direct opposition to ascetic Christian ideals, 'wild' people were seen as voraciously sexual creatures. The non-European man had a huge sexual appetite, the 'wild woman' was a sex nymph. 'Wild men, like the other representatives of the earth's monstrous races, had inhabited the Near Eastern and Western imaginations for millennia' (Stannard, 1992: 169); the Turks, the quintessence of Islam in early Orientalist accounts, for example, were represented as 'so much given to sodomy that "they loathe the natural use of the woman"' (Al-Azmeh, 1993: 124). Sneering and condemnatory accounts of the sexual and moral behaviour of Muslim men abound in European literary and scholarly accounts. The Oriental man is criticized and scorned for his 'lazy manner of living' and 'enslavement of women'. He has no other occupation than sitting around whole days, 'drinking coffee, Smoking Tobacco, or Eating, Drinking and Sleeping' (cited in Lowe, 1991: 38–9).

In recent years, several remarkable colonial discourse studies have interrogated the indulgence of French and English travel literature with the erotic Oriental Other. Judy Mabro, for example, has observed how strongly and consistently the descriptions of Middle Eastern people and societies were implicated by the images of the *Arabian Nights*. These images were applied indiscriminately to a large geographical area when these travellers found themselves anywhere in the Middle East (Mabro, 1996: 28).

In another study of the European travel literature, Lisa Lowe has uncovered the sexual fantasies of male travellers. In the eyes of the European male viewer, the 'Muslim woman' was 'far more Oriental than the man'. '*La femme orientale*' – represented, for example, in Gustave Flaubert's letters – was 'a masculine fantasy of pure erotic service in the industrialized age of French imperialism.' *La femme orientale* generated sexual pleasure, but was 'impassive, undemanding, and insensate herself; her oriental mystery never failed to charm, her resources never exhausted' (Lowe, 1991: 76). Unfettered by a reality that might not fit this imagery, the Western male viewer

constructed a pleasing image of Muslim woman, the enslaved source
of sexual pleasure and sexual possession, through 'studio fantasies',
often using prostitutes as models (Alloula, 1986; Graham-Brown,
1988).

The domesticated, subjugated, unenlightened Other as opposed
to the liberated, independent and enlightened Western self was used
as a moral prop to legitimize colonial power relations. Lisa Lowe's
examination of the writings of prominent men of literature and
philosophy in eighteenth- and nineteenth-century Europe, such as
Montesquieu's *Lettres Persiennes*, uncovers the persistent opposition of
Occident and Orient together with a discourse which attaches class
hierarchy and unequal gender relations. Thus, Persia in Montesquieu's
*Lettres* was to be 'the constructed opposite of France: the tyranny of
Persian harem contrasts with French representative government; the
cruel instinct of the Persian master and his eunuch guards opposes
French rationalism and law; and the confined chastity of the Persian
wives counters the freedom and infidelity of French women' (Lowe,
1991: 55).

Remarkably, female domesticity, and sexual purity and chastity,
deemed appropriate in Europe and aggressively promoted at home,
were presented for Muslim women as 'evidence' of sexual slavery
and signs of a peculiar moral and religious deficiency of the Other.
The point is not whether the imagery of Muslim women's role and
status corresponded to the reality, but rather that female 'sexual
slavery' and domesticity were not completely out of tune with
Western Christian values, explicit in the writings of men of literature
and philosophy like Jean-Jacques Rousseau and Arthur Schopenhauer.
Rousseau thought that to cure women from the ill qualities of indo-
lence and indocility, girls should be early subjected to restraints:
'They must be subject, all their lives, to the most constant and
severe restraint.' He suggested that to make girls more readily submit
to the will of others in their later lives it was necessary 'to accustom
them early to such confinements' (Osborne, 1979: 113). Schopenhauer considered woman to be 'weaker in her power of reasoning,
narrow in her vision, intellectually shortsighted, with no sense of
justice and inclination to extravagant to a length that borders mad-
ness'. All this, however, Schopenhauer suggested, fitted women 'to

amuse man in his hours of recreation, and in case of need, to console him when he is borne down by the weight of his cares' (Osborne, 1979: 213–14).

The condemnation of Islam for its treatment of women, curiously combined with a continuing indulgence of the signifier of female enslavement (the harem, the veil, polygamy), helped obscure and legitimize sexual and cultural repression of women in Europe, their non-person status and the sexual double standard. The European male establishment also appropriated feminism and used it against other cultures. This 'colonial feminism', as Leila Ahmed has remarked, was to legitimize Europe's 'civilizing mission'. Lord Cromer's words and actions in this area provide a glaring example. On the home front, against white men, feminism was to be resisted and suppressed; but it could be taken abroad, and directed against the cultures of colonized men. Ahmed's study reveals a curious paradox in Cromer's gender politics in Egypt and in England. Lord Cromer condemned Islam 'first and foremost' for its treatment of women; to attain mental and moral development, Egypt must abandon women's seclusion and the veil. In England, however, Cromer was a 'founding member and sometime President of the Men's League for Opposing Women's Suffrage'(L. Ahmed, 1992: 153). Women's subordination would continue at the centre of Empire, but the idea that Other men – men in colonized societies or in societies beyond the borders of the civilized West – oppressed women was used 'to render morally justifiable its project of undermining or eradicating the cultures of colonized people' (L. Ahmed, 1992: 51–153). Against the colonial backdrop, the role and status of the Muslim woman would become a stick with which the West could beat the East (Malti-Douglas, 1991: 3). The Muslim woman was to be exploited by the Western man but protected from enslavement by the Muslim man; she was to be liberated from her own ignorance and her culture's cruelty.

The question, however, is if Islam is not any more obsessed with human sexuality and female sexual purity than other religions, why is female sexuality so tightly linked with communal honour and politics in Islamic cultures? What are the socio-historical structures and processes which legitimize the regulation of female sexual and moral conduct by Islamic states? According to one argument, the blame must be laid at the door of European colonialism. The colonial construction of 'Muslim woman', her sexuality, sexual power and sexual enslavement, could cause cultural anxiety and rage in the Muslim man. The 'civilizing' and 'liberating' colonial policies in the area of women's rights would inevitably further aggravate the Muslim male, the colonized. Hiding women from the gaze of the Western viewer, and guarding women's bodies and their minds from changes produced by foreign intervention, symbolized protection of Islamic identity, communal dignity and social and cultural continuity. Which is to say that perhaps the resistance of Islamic societies to changing women's familial status is the reaction of a culture that has been shamelessly stereotyped and inferiorized like none other for its treatment of women. Hence, on this view, it was colonialism which made the 'Muslim woman' and her rights central to its imperial policy in the Middle East.

However, I consider problematic the argument which tries to justify the resistance of Islamic societies to changing women's familial status as a cultural reaction to colonialism. This over-emphasis on the role of colonialism is as inconclusive and debatable as the totalizing and universalizing approach which looks only to Qur'anic injunctions and Shari'a laws to explain the surveillance of women in Islamic societies, disregarding the basic fact that Islam, like any other religion or ideology, has a contingent nature and is the product of its articulation with indigenous cultures and societies. In fact, the spatio-temporal existence of Islam points to the heterogeneity of 'Islamic culture'. The idea of Islam as a kind of meta-culture obscures the reality that, as Aziz Al-Azmeh has noted, there are as many Islams as the conditions that sustain them – as many 'Islamic cultures' as different geographical, social conditions, size of wealth and educational levels can produce (Al-Azmeh, 1993: 6–8). That is to say, the similarities among Islamic societies in the application of principles of Shari'a, therefore, should not cloud significant differences between various interpretations of the Qur'an and the Shari'a in different time frames and in different settings, and the political context which determines the extent of their observance. For instance, polygamy, taken as Islam's engendering signifier, is prohibited in some countries in the Muslim world, such as Turkey and

Tunisia; the temporary marriage, *mut'a*,[1] a practice limited only to the Shi'i *Shari'a*, allowing a man to 'marry' as many women as he wishes for a set time and price, is strictly prohibited among the Shi'i Ismailis of East Africa. The Constitution of Shi'i Imami Ismailis, in fact, provides that a marriage 'may be solemnized between two members of the community only if neither party has a spouse living at the time of marriage' (Anderson, 1976: 110–11). Likewise, there are differences among Shi'i and Sunni Maliki, Hanbali and Hanafi schools of law on such issues as compulsory marriage and child marriage, that is, a guardian's right to contract a marriage on behalf of his minor ward.

Indeed, the relative variance in a religious and political tradition, stretching from Indonesia and Malaysia to Morocco, suggests that Islamic traditions and values could be accommodating and mouldable in proportion to the strength of local customs and cultural practices and to the processes of social and economic development. Nigerian Islam, which represents an accommodation between *Shari'a* injunctions and pre-Islamic African customs and mores, is different from the secularized Islamic practices in Azerbaijan where Islam represents a cultural-ethnic identity rather than a way of life. The impact of seventy years of Soviet legislation and secular social policies on Azerbaijan is that nearly all adult women work at salaried jobs, people eat pork and drink alcohol, and few Muslims are well-informed about Islam (Dragadze, 1994: 156–62). Both Nigerian and Azarbaijani Islams have significant differences with Khomeinist Islam in Iran, where state legislation, invoking *Shari'a* interpretations, invent 'Islamic' rules to further restrict women's physical mobility and participation in public life. The existence of different Islams practised in the Muslim world means that the local customs and practices, urf, have made effective contributions in the stipulation of personal status legislation within territorial borders. Hence, Islam cannot be taken, perhaps, as the sole signifier of the situation of women in Islamic societies. Even under Islamic rule, class and wealth, to a great extent, define women's life options and gender experience.

Moreover, colonial rule in other parts of the world also involved the invention of stereotypical images for the native population, the brutal abuse of female sexuality, and sexual objectification and

exploitation of native women. Everywhere women and the con-
quered territories 'were concurrently exploited as part of the bounty
due to the conquering Europeans'. For example, the myth about the
'New World' was that there were 'young and beautiful women, who
everywhere were naked, in most places accessible, and presumably
complaisant' (Atkinson, 1992: 88, 5–9). However, in the Americas
we cannot see the stubborn resistance to change the legal status of
women after the fall of colonialism that we observe in Islamic
societies.

Furthermore, the patterns of colonization by European powers
were different in different parts of the Islamic world. Yet Islamic
societies, with some exceptions, over many centuries, disclose greater
similarities than differences in their rigidity in the treatment of
women, particularly in the area of women's legal rights and personal
status – as illustrated, for example, in making provisions of the
Shari'a the bases of women's legal rights in personal status and legislation pertaining to marriage and divorce, inheritance, custody – all
of which define and confine women's participation in social and
political activities. There were substantial differences between the
lengthy occupation of Algeria by the French and the 'civilizing' and
'Frenchifying' policies of the colonizer – specifically targeting Muslim
women – and the relatively short presence of the British in Egypt,
where the power of local rulers and Ottoman legal traditions remained virtually intact. Still, in both cases women's status and rights,
to varying extents, remained within the confines of the Shari'a.

The point is that colonial or home-grown, externally imposed or
locally generated, compelled by Qur'anic injunctions and Shari'a
rulings or the erratic interpretations of local ulama, 'Muslim woman',
her sexuality and her moral conduct, has remained a central preoccupation of Muslim men over many centuries. This preoccupation
has been translated into institutions, policies, legal practices and
personal status codes which determine women's life options and the
extent of women's participation in public life. Which is to say that
despite the capacity of Islam to adapt and to change face and force
under the influence of various social, political and economic stimuli,
the systematic, vigorous and often violent opposition to change is
a grim reality in many Islamic societies.

Of course in almost all human societies cultural beliefs surrounding female sexuality, perceived as the site of motherhood, wifehood, fertility, purity, modesty and selflessness, construct beliefs and values pertaining to differing feminine and masculine roles and gender relations. However, female sexuality (or the control and the protection of it) finds a more complex political meaning in Islamic societies. Seen as the symbol of Islamic social order and cultural continuity, restraining and disciplining female sexuality seems to draw the boundaries between 'Muslim culture' and non-Muslim Other.

## The Islamic Concept of Sexuality

In Islamic societies, the woman's body generates fascination and pleasure. It is exploited for procreation, and as a symbol of communal dignity. It is manipulated and its activities are codified. It is covered and confined. It is disciplined for defiance and is mutilated in anticipation of trespassing – all this often sanctioned legally and, particularly, culturally. The female body is the site of struggle between the proponents and opponents of modernity and is used as a playing card between imperial and anti-imperial political forces. In Islamic societies, sexuality, the site of love, desire, sexual fulfilment and physical procreation, is, at the same time, for women, the site of shame, confinement, anxiety, compulsion. 'With the first drop of her menstrual blood, every Muslim girl becomes a temple of her family's honor' (Minai, 1981: 100). Woman's expression of her desires and the pursuit of her interests contradicts the interests of man and challenges man's God-given rights over woman. Underpinning the sexual and moral beliefs and practices in Islamic societies is the conception of woman as weak in moral judgement and deficient in cognitive capacity, yet sexually forceful and irresistibly seductive. The susceptibility of women to corruption, in this view, explains the obsession with sexual purity in Islamic cultures and justifies surveillance of women by family, community and state.

Managed independent of her desire and will, sexuality for women becomes the legal possession of the Islamic community, umma, and, by extension, of the state. Laws pertaining to marriage and divorce speak clearly of women's disabilities in enjoying full legal status. The marriage contract and the termination of it, divorce, are negotiated between the state and male citizens, that is, father in the case of marriage, and husband in the case of divorce. Young virgin women, according to the Islamic *Shari'a*, need the permission of their fathers or guardians to enter a marriage contract; fathers can legally marry off their under-age daughters for a set price, *mahr*; and a man can end the marriage contract without the consent or even the knowledge of his wife. The diverging interpretations of Qur'anic rulings and various legal traditions and reforms launched in Islamic societies in the area of personal status have done little to remove women's legal disabilities in marriage and divorce.

Do these facts speak to the unchanging character of the Islamic conception of sexuality and its essential difference from other traditional religions in this area? Although different interpretations and traditions within Islam makes it hard to generalize, it can be said that Islam is a sex-affirming cultural and religious tradition. The Islamic attitude towards sexual pleasure may, indeed, be a major dividing line between Islam and other traditional religions. Strictly interpreted, both Judaism and Christianity approve of sexual relations between man and woman, but only in marriage and only in the service of procreation. Historically, both Judaism (which was not ascetic and encouraged marriage and procreation) and Christianity (which celebrates celibacy and virginity – because marriage is a worldly obligation which might interfere with devotion to God) – condemn any kind of sex that did not lead to reproduction. Sexual pleasure was a sin, in early Christianity, if children were not the object (Tannahill, 1989: 153). Christians even promoted the idea of sexless marriage – that is, the sexual union of a couple which was legally and religiously sanctioned should not be 'infected' by lust (Bullough, 1976).

Islam, by contrast, disapproves of celibacy. The Prophet is believed to have considered marriage for a Muslim as half of his religion. Marriage, according to Maliki and Hanafi schools, is obligatory for men. Marriage shields them from 'promiscuity, adultery, fornication, homosexuality', and is commendable 'even for a person who has strong will to control his sexual desire, who has no wish to have

children, and who feels that marriage will keep him away from his
devotion to Allah' (Doi Abdul Rahman, 1989: 33–4). Islam opposes
celibacy and celebrates sexual pleasure as a legitimate right of the
believer. Sex in itself is regarded as a sacred function within the
domestic field. For this reason, the Prophet paid special attention to
the relations between a man and his wife. The promises made to the
believer of the 'good life' awaiting him in Paradise, a space in which
sexual indulgence with 'eternally young', 'fair' and 'wide-eyed'
women seems to be man's only activity, can, perhaps, expose what
constituted ultimate happiness for the Muslim believer (Sabbah, 1988:
91–7). Eternally lasting physical pleasure and unrestricted access to
the female body as the source of physical pleasure would be deliv-
ered to the believing man in Paradise as rewards for his piety, good
deeds and self-control in life. Decoding Islamic Paradise, Fatna Sabbah
suggests that the paradisal female model, the huri, represents the
ideal female and, at the same time, the ideal society for the Muslim
believer. The huri 'is created to be consumed as a sexual partner, her
value comes from her physical beauty, which God gives as a gift to
the believer'. She is passive and is stripped of the human dimen-
sion. 'She has been created for one sole destiny: to be consumed by
the male believer' (Sabbah, 1988: 96–7). Given the fact that, as will
shortly be discussed, religious instructions in Islamic societies are at
the same time state legislation, this concept of sexuality has specific
legal consequences for women.

While approving of sexual pleasure, the Islamic orthodox view
develops, at the same time, a justification for sexual hierarchy, with
women as sexual objects at the service of men. The Qur'an makes
men 'the managers of the affairs of women', requiring righteous
women to be 'obedient, guarding the secret for God's guarding',
advising women to 'cast down their eyes, guard their private parts
and reveal not their adornment ... save to their husbands'. The sure
outcome of this palpable sexual hierarchy, incorporated into family
laws in Islamic societies, is that woman's very existence is serving
men, sexually and emotionally. Women are a 'tillage' for the male
believer, to go to when he wishes. If a wife refuses her husband's
sexual demands, she is to be punished.[2]

The Shi'i jurisdiction in Iran, for example, lays down the rights and obligation of women, based on the view that it is the woman's religious duty to submit to all sexual demands of her husband. Ayatollah Khomeini clarifies this point beyond any doubt: 'A woman who has been contracted permanently, must not leave the house without the husband's permission and must surrender herself for any pleasure that he wants and must not prevent him from having intercourse with her without a religious excuse' (Khomeini, 1980: 318). He further makes the ruling that: 'If the wife does not obey her husband in those actions mentioned in [the] previous problem, she is a sinner and has no right to food and clothing and shelter.' In the Sunni tradition also a married woman has the obligation to be faithful and obedient to her husband and to admit him to sexual intercourse (when he so desires) (Chaudhry, 1991: 34).

In the end, Islam's hierarchical concept of sexuality, coupled with gender discrimination in the realm of sexual love and desire, means that even though – unlike other traditional religions – Islam recognizes sexual desires and the need for their fulfilment for both sexes, it makes it harder in practice for women to achieve sexual satisfaction. Female sexual drives and women's right to sexual fulfilment through the institution of marriage is recognized and legally sanctioned in Islamic tradition. A married woman has the right to sexual fulfilment and the husband is required to respect that right by not abandoning intercourse with his wife for more than four months. Yet the Muslim man, it is presumed, has sexual drives that cannot be satisfied with only one woman at a time. Therefore, he is allowed to marry four women and hire as many temporary 'wives' as he can afford, through the institution of mut'a (temporary marriage) – as is still the case in Shi'i tradition. This special allowance made to men in effect nullifies women's right to sexual pleasure as recognized in Islam. Since Islam strongly discourages solitary sex and severely punishes homosexuality, marriage is the only permissible framework within which women can seek sexual pleasure. In polygamous union, women's rights to sexual pleasure are confined to one quarter of a man.

This apparent contradiction in Islamic views of female sexuality may be the root cause of Islam's obsessive concern with the rights and wrongs of female sexual conduct. No doubt, in a tradition that looks with disfavour on 'illegitimate' children, the importance of ensuring physical paternity and an unconfused bloodline is an important reason for the surveillance of women's moral conduct. Yet it is Muslim men's explicit and implicit fear of female sexuality and women's seductive power which explains the seclusion and surveillance of women in Islamic cultures (Mernissi, 1985: 30–1). For, if female sexuality is seen as active but a woman's movements for fulfilment of her desires are forcefully restrained, sexual transgression may appear to be inevitable. Moreover, since a man may be expected not to have much control over his sexual desires, men are understood as victims of female seductive power.

The fear of the intensity of female sexual desire and her seductive power, indeed, viewing woman-as-body and an exclusive physical entity, as Fatna Sabbah argues, is explicit in both Islamic legal discourse and particularly in erotic discourse. The likelihood of discharge of woman's sexual energy that no man can possibly resist is the source of men's anxiety for two reasons. First, it makes men preoccupied with sexual performance, with prolonging intercourse and with searching for a sexual strategy that can meet female expectations in bed. Hence, sexual relations constitute a continuing crisis for the believer, because they divert attention from God (Sabbah, 1988: 50, 90). Second, women's seductive power is a threat to Muslim social order. Woman, in Imam Ali's words, is wholly evil; and the worst thing about her is that she is a necessary evil (Bouhdiba, 1985: 117). She is necessary because, as expressed in the Qur'an, her womb is a field that can cultivate the seeds of man. The prominent interpreters of the Qur'an, like Imam Ghazali, saw women's power as the most destructive element in the Muslim social order.

It should go without saying that the fear of women's seductive power is not unique to Islam. In Jewish scriptural and oral (Talmud) tradition, practised, particularly, by the minority Hasidics, women seem to have an aggressive and insatiable sexual drive to the extent that men are only willing victims of women's enticement. Likewise, the Christian Fathers saw women at fault for causing male sexual arousal. In fact St Paul believed that women's seductive powers were so great that they caused even angels to sin (Bullough, 1976: 76, 178–9). The grip of these statements over sexual morality in Western civilization is well known. Nonetheless, in the West the standards of sexual morality and immorality in private which do not harm or cause offence to other persons are not normally enforced by law. For example, sexual relationship outside marriage is not a legal offence unless it is aggravated by circumstances such as lack of consent or rape or when it involves sex with an under-age person. Islamic law, by contrast, holds that any sexual relationship is a crime unless it is between husband and wife (Coulson, 1969: 77–8). This distinction endows Islamic morality with a more paralysing impact for the lives of women (and men). Religious moral instruction and standards constitute the bases of women's legal rights and personal status. The observance of Islamic moral standards is enforced by law.

The Christian Fathers, except for a short period, were not states-men. They, of course, manipulated the state to enhance their own power and influence, as well as the influence of their faith. But social, economic and political developments in European societies, including the establishment of the modern legal system, recognition of the rights of the individual *vis-à-vis* the state, universal suffrage and equality before the law, in different historical periods in various European countries, diminished the arbitrary power of the Christian church and the possibility for it to manipulate the state and the courts to enforce its vision of moral and immoral conduct on the citizenry. With the separation of church from state, the rule of law in the West was substituted for the rule of the divine. This opened the space for the formation of a relatively strong civil society – a crucial development towards accountability of the state. These developments have been instrumental in the struggle of women in European societies for gender equity and justice.

In the case of Judaism, the experience of Jewishness for women, one would think, has been, and is still, different depending on to which denomination (Ultra-Orthodox, Conservative or Reform) they belong or in which part of the world they live, as well as on the class status of members of the Jewish community. In the state of Israel, Orthodox movements have historically used the state both to gain more resources for their institutions and to impose as many religious practices as possible on Israeli society (Yuval-Davis, 1992: 206). Israeli women's legal rights in matters of marriage and divorce have been shaped in the process of the cooperation and compromises made between the nationalistic (and militaristic) goals of the state and the patriarchal values of Jewish Orthodoxy – vehemently defended by the Orthodox coalitions in parliament. The articulation of Jewish patriarchal values (which regard women not as individual citizens with distinct interests and needs, but primarily as the guardians of Jewish home – wives – and producers of future generations of Jews – mothers) with the 'security' needs of the state of Israel has resulted in compromising secular principles at the expense of women. The enactment of the 1953 Marriage and Divorce Law (ending civil marriage and divorce by the recognition of the authority of Rabbinical Courts in these matters) is a case in point (Jorgensen, 1994: 285–7; Landau, 1993: 127–32). However, the state never assumed the responsibility of overseeing women's moral conduct. Observing the 'right Jewish way', which involves following rigid religious instructions in every sphere of life has, to a large extent, remained a personal choice that individuals make in order to be part of a specific Orthodox or Ultra-Orthodox group.

Islam, however, is a religion as well as a legal and political tradition. It also embodies sexual moral and ethical principles which are strictly enforced. The spiritual leaders in Islamic tradition have been, at the same time, the legislators and administrators of the affairs of the Muslim community. Statements and instructions of Islamic Fathers relating to sexual morality and women's personal conduct are not to be traced only in orthodox Islamic texts or practices of Muslim fanatics. They are principles which are enforced through the criminal legal system. Sexual offences in Islamic cultures must be understood in this context.

The fear of female sexuality and concerns over women's moral conducts are not, therefore, limited to orthodox views of bygone generations. Ayatollah Motahhari's writings in pre-revolutionary Iran, for example, demonstrated his deep concerns over the presence of unveiled women and its 'disastrous' effect on Iranian youth. Women, he thought, 'were turning the youth, who should be the symbol of strength, will-power and productivity, into weak, pleasure-seeking and lustful oglers' (Motahhari, 1358/1979: 91–3). Fearing the tempting power of female sexuality, Motahhari argued in favour of making the veil mandatory in the institutions of higher education. The appearance of unveiled women in educational institutions, offices and factories, Motahhari thought, is sexually provocative and diverts men's attention from productive activities. Motahhari was not convinced that even *hejab* could curb women's sexual and seductive power, for he suggested that female and male students in universities should be separated in classrooms by a curtain. The suggestion was put into practice in post-revolutionary Iran.

It should go without saying that Motahhari's ideas are typical of arguments by Muslim conservatives in the Islamic world. Opposing Western ideals of human rights, Abul Ala Mawdudi in Pakistan, for example, considers the preservation of women's chastity through purdah to be one of the 'basic principles of human rights in the Islamic world' (cited in Mayer, 1995: 100–1). He instructed that 'women should wrap themselves up well in their sheets, and should draw and let down a part of the sheet in front of the face'. Another Islamic jurist in Pakistan, Justice Aftab Hussain, argues that purdah keeps both sexes chaste and avoids them gazing at one another (Chaudhry, 1991: 107–8). Nonetheless, it needs to be emphasized that while all Islamic conservatives advocate *hejab* or purdah for women, they do not agree, necessarily, on the idea of domesticity for them. Moreover, despite the influence of the rhetoric of domesticity, Islamic movements and states, in practice, draw women to public life, albeit within all-female networks and essentially in the service of the sexual segregation of public life (Gruenbaum, 1992; Moghissi, 1995; Tessler and Jesse, 1996).

The Islamic idea that women have a pernicious seductive power which endangers the Muslim social order, when translated into laws and legal practices, affects the believer and non-believer, Muslims and non-Muslims alike. Thus, Islamists, whether as functionaries of the state or members of the Islamic *umma* (community), take upon themselves the guardianship of the moral purity of women in their societies. Indeed, the Islamic principle of *amr-i bi marouf va nahy-i az monkar* (ordering good and preventing evil) rules out any recognition and respect for the concept of individual right to choice and equal protection under the law. In this context, the clutches of the guardians of the Islamic *Shari'a* are felt in every aspect of women's (and men's) lives. For instance, in Saudi Arabia women are barred from driving. In Sudan, middle-class professional women, seen as the 'same as prostitutes', are harassed and questioned by the regime, as well as by self-appointed 'moral guards', about their presence in public and their relationships to the men in their company (Hale, 1996: 192). In Iran, the Head of Islamic Police in Tehran rules that women are not 'to smile at strange men, because a woman's smile might arouse satanic lust'.[3] These practices take their legitimacy from the idea that female sexuality has to be confined, tamed and controlled for the good of the community. The state's control over women's moral conduct, therefore, goes so far as policing women's movement, looks and smiles in public.

These realities raise several questions as to what cultural and religious suppositions and what complex socio-cultural and political circumstances sustain the formidable influence and authority of Islamic laws, and traditions perceived as Islamic, over women's lives. What are the psychological impulses and mental frames in Islamic cultures which tolerate or even license the violent disciplining by men of female sexual and moral conduct? These questions, in the end, must merge with the problematic of the rise of Islamic fundamentalist movements in contemporary Middle Eastern and North African societies.

Indeed, the ideological construction of female sexuality as the symbolic representation of Muslim identity and its centrality in the fundamentalists' 'cultural purification' schemes means that women lose much more than men do in the process of Islamization of the already Muslim societies. The legal sanctioning of various forms of gender violence is the most immediate consequence for women of Islamization schemes. Revitalization of ancient (and often bizarre) legal practices, such as stoning of women accused of *zena* (extramarital relations), reduces women's legal status and promotes hostility towards them. The provisions of the 1979 Hudud Ordinance (Islamic criminal punishments) and the Law of Evidence, introduced by Zia ul-Haq in Pakistan, for example, specifically affected women. The part of the Ordinance which affected women most seriously was *zena*, which encompasses both extramarital sex and rape. A man and a woman accused of *zena* were sentenced to death by stoning or a hundred lashes. The same provision also was applied to the case of rape. To determine whether the case before court was *zena* or rape (that is, whether or not the women consented to sex), the court required either the confession by the rapist or the presence of four morally 'trustworthy' Muslim men. By prescribing that there must be four Muslim male adults as eyewitnesses, the law excludes the testimony of women altogether, even in the case of their own rape. Moreover, by blurring the line between *zena* and rape, and given the fact that, even in modern legal systems, establishing the guilt of a rapist is difficult, Zia's 1979 law ended up discriminating against women and helping rapists to get off the hook (Haq, 1996: 158–75; Mumtaz and Shaheed, 1987: 100–6). Hence, among women who received public lashes and were fined and imprisoned at the time was a blind domestic servant, Safia, who had survived multiple rapes by her employer. The legislators of this cruel ruling leave no room for doubt that in their view women are to blame for sexual crimes committed against them.

Similarly, the move to 'Islamize' the already Islamic Sudan, starting with Numeiri's declaration of Sudan as an Islamic Republic and its strict adherence to the *Shari'a* in 1983, particularly affected women. With the passage of the Islamic penal code, for example, the Numeiri regime dropped the law against infibulation which was passed under British rule and had remained on the books until 1983. The Islamization policy was further intensified under the fundamentalist military junta after Numeiri's downfall in 1989. Among the first Islamic acts of the revolutionary government were the curtailing of women's freedom of movement and the imposition of the Islamic dress code, *hejab*, which followed the suspension of the constitution, outlawing all political parties, unions, and professional associations, and the imposition of the Islamic *Shari'a* on non-Muslims (Hale, 1996: 88–91, 111).

Within this context, it makes more sense to understand the plight of women in Islamic cultures as the combined impact of socio-historical economic and political retardation of Islamic societies and its articulation with indigenous customs and patriarchal cultural values which conspire to sustain the authority of misogynist religious commands over the lives of women. The non-separation of religion

and politics, the unclear divide in Islamic societies between law-
and policy-makers and religious-spiritual leaders, have smothered
the already weak civil society. In the majority of countries of the
Islamic world, civil society, which is the space for the formation
and contestation of progressive counter-hegemonic forces, has not
existed except in rare historical moments. The space for contestation
has been closed to women, religious minorities and progressive
secular forces. Religious leaders and political rulers – except when
their interests clash – equally benefit from the convergence of politics
and religion and from a stifled civil society. By giving a divine
character to political commands they try to protect themselves against
progressive radical challenges. It should go without saying that this
socio-political dynamism is not conducive to change in favour of
women.

In the end, ironically, Islamic fundamentalists, by embracing the
female body as the symbolic representation of communal dignity,
and by drawing only on the Qur'an and orthodox texts to explain,
as divine, the historically developed subjugation of women in Islamic
societies, recycle the totalizing colonial conception of Islam and
women's rights as a static, unchanging and unchangeable order. As
with other forms of extremism, the two opposing poles end up on
the same side on certain important issues. By manipulating the female
body as a playing card in oppositional politics, fundamentalists, in
fact, embrace, however unsought and uncomfortable, the views of
the Western colonizer.

## Notes

Some of the material in this chapter was used in my 'Women, Sexuality
and Social Policy in Islamic Cultures', *International Review of Comparative Public
Policy*, Vol. 9, 1997: 149–68.

   1.  Mut'a or temporary marriage, a pre-Islamic custom, is a verbal contract
between a man and a woman, who is *hired* to be the man's wife, for fixed
pay and for a fixed period. Termination of the *mut'a* contract does not
require divorce procedures. The man and the woman part when the contract
is expired or when the man so wishes, that is, if he relinquishes his rights
to the remaining period of the contract. Mut'a was forbidden after the
Prophet's death. The practice, however, continued through the centuries in
Shi'ite Iran. While mut'a is, essentially, a cheap and easy means for sexual

gratification and is widely considered a form of legal prostitution in Iran, it has also served other purposes in the past. For example, since any close contact between men and women outside marriage was prohibited except among immediate family members, mut'a was sometimes used to make non-sexual contact and friendship between men and women religiously and culturally acceptable. On the institution of mut'a, see Haeri (1989).

2. See Sura II: 223 (The Cow) in the Qur'an (Arberry, 1964).

3. See Iran Times, 17 June 1994.

# Chapter 2

# From Orientalism to Islamic Feminism

Of all the regions of the 'East', it is only Islamic societies that have been conceptualized almost completely in terms of the determinative role of religion. Only under Islam, its Orientalist version, does religion appear as an organizing force, shaping all aspects of society. Farsoun and Hajjar note that while all three traditional religions, Judaism, Christianity and Islam, might be said to provide blueprints for social order, 'societies that profess Christianity are not analyzed as Christian societies.' Israel is usually analysed as a 'secular society', although also commonly referred to as 'the Jewish state'. It is only Middle Eastern history that 'is conventionally viewed as the history of Islam', and only Islam which has 'an air of static, eternal permanence, uninfluenced by historical change, except, perhaps, the consequence of external factors, such as contact with the West' (Farsoun and Hajjar, 1990: 164).

As I discussed in Chapter 1, religion played a definitive role also in explaining women's status in Muslim societies. In fact, the constructed oppression of 'Muslim women' was central to what Edward Said has identified as the Orientalization of the Middle East. That is, the representation of the Oriental Other as the opposite of the European – a polarizing distinction between West and East. Said does not deny real differences in human realities, as expressed in different cultural practices and social mores. Indeed, human societies, argues Said, are divided into clearly different cultures, histories, traditions, societies, even races. But as a form of thought,

Orientalism seized upon such divisions, historically and actually, to 'press the importance of the distinction between some men and some other men'. Orientalism essentialized a radical difference between Western superiority and Oriental inferiority, 'between the familiar (Europe, the West, "us") and the strange (the Orient, the East, "them")'; it expressed 'the strength of the West and the Orient's weakness'. This gave the West legitimate authority not only to represent the Orient but to change its reality. It conferred upon the West a 'civilizing mission' in the Orient (Said, 1978: 42–5).

Said did not suggest that the 'Orient was *essentially* an idea, or a creation with no corresponding reality', but that the phenomenon of Orientalism does deal principally with the ideas of Orientalists about the Orient, 'despite or beyond any correspondence'. It was the 'intellectual power' which allowed Europeans to deal with and even to see Orientals as a phenomenon possessing regular characteristics, which set them apart from Europeans. 'Control of the Other through knowledge' is the central component of Said's argument (Turner, 1994: 96). Said drew attention to the fact that writings on Islamic societies and cultures originated in a particular context – the political, economic and professional interests involved in the representation of Arabs, Persians and Muslims, in general, and their cultural practices as exercised in Western literature and scholarly writings. Another key point is that the line separating Occident from Orient is a human production, not a fact of nature. It is an 'imaginative geography'.

Said's *Orientalism* and other writings of similar intellectual and political force (like Talal Asad's *The Idea of an Anthropology of Islam* [1968] and Thierry Hentsch's *Imagining the Middle East* [1992]) impress upon the reader that 'the Orient' which was represented in Western philosophical and literary writings was 'at least from the 19th century onward, an Orient of dreams, victim of power politics and product of imagination' (Hentsch, 1992: 119). Thus, the Orient was Orientalized, not only because it was discovered to be 'Oriental', but because it 'could be – that is, submitted to being – made Oriental' (Said, 1978: 6). This close link between power and knowledge in the discourse of representation is central to the discussion of Orientalism. This is how, for example, Said read Flaubert's representation of the Oriental Muslim woman:

> Flaubert's encounter with an Egyptian courtesan produced a widely in-
> fluential model of the Oriental woman; she never spoke of herself, she
> never represented her emotions, presence, or history. He spoke for and
> represented her. He was foreign, comparatively wealthy, male, and these
> were historical facts of domination that allowed him not only to possess
> Kuchuk Hanem physically but to speak for her and tell his readers in
> what way she was 'typically Oriental'. (Said, 1978: 6)

And it is in this complex context that still powerful anti-Arab, anti-
Iranian and anti-Muslim feelings and prejudices are better understood.

Said's *Orientalism* has been the subject of critical analyses and close
scrutiny, often with the same scholarly rigour as his own. He has
been criticized for his Orientalism-in-reverse (Al-Azm, 1981: 367–
71), for being ahistorical, inconsistent and nativist, and for falsifying
Islam, to name only a few charges to which he has responded (Said,
1985).[1] Said has also been criticized for having difficulty 'in extract-
ing himself from the skin of the victim'. It is claimed that he has
used the guilty conscience of Western intellectuals to silence them
(Hentsch, 1992: 189, 193). To be sure, Said's critique of the West's
representation of Muslims and Arabs and, more generally, of Islamic
civilization was not a novelty. Scholars like Maxime Rodinson (1973),
Talal Asad (1973) and Hamid Enayat (1973) in the Anglophone
academy had already tried to deconstruct Orientalist myths about
the Islamic world. But Said's careful analysis of Orientalist colonial
discourses opened a new political and scholarly terrain. Said generated a new alertness to the pitfalls of representational works, thus
inspiring greater sensitivity in appraising the West's view of the
Middle East and enlivening younger scholars working in the areas
of nationalism, post-colonialism, anti-racism, identity and representation. I suspect the Indian scholar Partha Chatterjee spoke for many
who felt the book said 'what one had always wanted to say' and had
talked of things one 'had known all along but had never found the
language to formulate with clarity' (Chatterjee, 1992: 195). Said's
*Orientalism* and other anti-Orientalist scholarly works did not specifically deal with gender. But they created or ratified in this area, as
in others, what Bruce Robbins (1992: 49–50) has called an 'anti-
representational common sense', leading to an almost 'uncontested
ethnico-epistemological denial of anyone's right or ability to represent *others*'.

## A Breakthrough in Studies of Gender and Islam

The anti-Orientalist trend found a welcome home among scholars of the Middle East and of gender and Islamic studies. Feminists analysing colonial discourse launched a counter-hegemonic argument, claiming, for example, that the stubborn survival of such practices as *hejab* and gender segregation and seclusion – the pre-eminent signifier of Islamic maltreatment of women – was, in fact, closely linked with the colonial presence in the region, at least in Islamic societies such as Iran, Egypt and Algeria. Some of these studies also challenged the positive impact presumed for European capitalism in promoting women's economic activities. They suggested, for example, that by undermining economic activities such as the artisan production of textiles, European capitalism, in fact, hurt female merchants throughout the area (L. Ahmed, 1992; Cole, 1981; Hatem, 1986; Keddie and Bonnie, 1981; Sayigh, 1981; Smith, 1984).

Colonialism, feminists argued, by making the Muslim woman and her rights central to imperial policy in the Middle East, sharply reduced Muslim identity to the control of women's moral conduct and their appearance in colonized Islamic lands. Hiding women from the Western gaze, and guarding women's bodies and their minds from changes produced by foreign intervention, came to symbolize protection of Islamic identity, communal dignity and social and cultural continuity. In this way, ironically, the 'civilizing' and 'liberating' gender policies of colonial powers may have proved counter-productive, creating more resistance than would have been otherwise the case. French rule in Algeria, for example, by using prostitution as a means of social coercion, targeted families unwilling to collaborate with the new ruler; it gave nationalism and the de-colonization movement a distinctively gendered character – mobilizing additional cultural and religious energies (Lazreg, 1994: 55). Studies of gender relations in the Middle East responded to an urgent gap in the literature in the area. They make a decisive break with the previous writings which, except for a few pioneering works on Middle Eastern economy, nearly exclusively focused on 'Islamic' history, Islamic values and ideas. Still, as Tucker puts it, we face a kind of 'ghettoization of women's history'. Social historians write about diverse issues and classes in the Middle East but rarely do we see in these works any consistent reflection on gender issues. Women are mentioned only in passing (Tucker, 1990: 198–227). Nonetheless, there are certainly more scholars today who write on women and gender in the Middle East, and many more who are interested in the subject. As Simona Sharoni has observed, the mere number of publications, papers and conferences on gender and women indicate that the field is moving closer to the centre of the research and teaching agenda in Middle East studies (Sharoni, 1997: 28).

With the rise of Islamic fundamentalism to political prominence in the late 1970s and early 1980s and the subsequent developments in world politics, a new wave of Islamophobia struck the West. Those were difficult years. Iran's 1979 Revolution against the Shah and the assassination in Egypt two years later of President Anwar el-Sadat dethroned the West's two powerful 'modern' allies in the region. Both events were the result of actions by Islamists, or, at least, with the Islamists' operative intervention. The United States and Israel, its closest ally in the region, were directly challenged by the takeover of the American Embassy in Tehran and by two militant Islamist populist movements: Hezbollah in Lebanon and, later, Hamas in the Occupied Territories. Then the Persian Gulf war unleashed vicious racist tropes in various Western countries, particularly in the United States against the Arab and Islamic worlds.

We can appreciate the extent of Islamophobia of the period and the 'controlling power' of constructed knowledge by recalling the endless news pieces, commentaries and reports, the racial humour and the use in talk shows of biblical metaphor and carefully fabricated 'facts' conjured up for the occasion about Arabs and Muslims; the crude imagery offered to justify the invasion of Iraq that revitalized the timeless opposition between the civilized and democratic West and the Islamic Orient; movies such as Not Without My Daughter (1991), which just happened to find screening about the same time as Operation Desert Storm – all this served to legitimize a brutal and cowardly war against the Iraqi 'sand nigger' and 'camel jockey'[2] and to make the unprotected Iraqi civilian population the target of 'smart bombs' and laser-guided weapons.

Trying to push from consciousness its colonial past, the West seemed in the grip of an overpowering urge to demonize the Muslims and Arabs for what it saw as the high-point of their difference with the West: 'Islamic' gender politics and practices. Once more the maltreatment of women and their exotic attire became the focal point of representational discourses on the Middle East, providing compelling evidence for the moral, cultural and political deficiencies of the Islamic world. The veil and sex segregation of public spaces in Iran and a few other Islamic societies made plausible the inferiorizing stereotypes and totalizing representation of Muslims and Arabs in general. Self-congratulatory discussions from a Western hegemonic position about women's rights 'here' as opposed to their deprivation 'there' worked to fuel everyday racism, somehow softening the shame of the West as a violent, clumsy bully.

To counter-balance or neutralize the growing arsenal of racist imagery launched against Muslims, Arabs and Iranians became a pressing necessity. The proliferation of publications, conferences and seminars on Islam and gender practices was the energetic response of scholars of the Middle East based in European and North American universities to the West's revitalized Islamophobia. The pressure of the political moment required and inspired more anti-representational and self-affirmative studies of gender and Islam. By surveying women's roles and statuses in various Islamic societies, a large number of sophisticated and enlightening publications, case studies, social histories and edited volumes called attention to the complexity and heterogeneity in Islamic societies of women's situations across class, ethnicity and diverse regional locations and to Middle Eastern women's strength, resilience and resistance. By exposing vested interests in colonial and stereotypical images of Islam and of Muslim women, these studies succeeded, to a large extent, in slowly changing the balance in favour of confirmative studies of women in Islamic societies, casting doubt on Orientalist and neo-Orientalist discourses.

However, these anti-Orientalist studies of gender and Islam now faced a daunting task. They needed to counter anti-Muslim prejudices and neo-Orientalist representation of Muslim women, without getting caught in an apologetic or self-denying defence of Islamic gender practices or a justification of the oppressive discourses and actions of Islamist ideologues and rulers.

## The Construction of a New 'Muslim Woman'

Generally, studies of women in the Middle East are moving in the right direction toward a more informed and sensitive understanding of the complexity of women's lives, decoding the colonialist, self-promoting Eurocentric representation of women in Islam societies. But I want to argue that sufficient attention has not been given to the inherent dangers in this, that is, overlooking the role of Islamic legal institutions and practices in maintaining, through the ages, the specific patriarchal order which circumscribes women's lives in Muslim societies.

A significant number of scholars in the field consider pre-existing patriarchal socio-cultural factors and internal economic structures and political systems (stifled or upheld by imperialist intervention and foreign interest) as the component elements of a male-centred network which impedes gender democracy and delineates prospects for real equity in Islamic societies. However, their analysis of the influence of Islam, refreshingly, is not void of the impact of other social realities in the Middle East, including global economic and political interests, and imperialist interventions which are conducive to the fundamentalist extravagances of various creeds. Most work in this genre does not focus only on what Suha Sabbagh calls a 'culture of misery', that is, reflecting 'a greater degree of domination than that actually exercised by men over women within Muslim culture' (Sabbagh, 1996: xiii), but emphasizes women's irrepressible strength and struggles rather than their victimization, thus not mystifying their life experiences under patriarchal Islamic legal and cultural traditions and institutions (Badran, 1994; Hale, 1996; Hatem, 1993; Imam, 1994; Kandiyoti 1991a, 1991b, 1995; Keddie and Baron, 1991; Mernissi, 1991, 1992, 1995; El Saadawi, 1997; Sabbagh, 1996). Many among this group draw attention to the inadequacy of the dominant discourse on women in the Middle East. Rejecting the monolithic and essentialist conceptions of both Islam and patriarchy, Kandiyoti, for example, argues that 'patriarchy' is an inadequate blanket term which cannot explain the articulation between Islam and different systems of male dominance, which are grounded in distinct material arrangements between genders. She places her emphasis on the variations in policies, legislation and practices, which represent 'the diverse cultural complexities' Islam encounters. The argument is that Islam is neither 'all there is to know', nor 'of little consequence in understanding the condition of women'. The historical articulation of Islam with classical-type patriarchy, which is grounded in distinct material social, political and cultural factors, determines the degree of women's access to education, employment and political participation in different societies (Kandiyoti, 1991b: 24). Hatem also stresses the need to 'deconstruct the categories of Islam, modernity, and women', and to 'begin a more fruitful discussion of the changing lives of women of different classes, of different ethnic groups, and different regions'. She argues that a limit has been reached to the dominant discourse on women in Islamic societies – shared by both modernist-nationalist and conservative-Islamists – that use 'Islamic/ Arab culture as a basis for their political legitimacy' and make women's rights a 'secondary commitment', thus crippling women in different ways (Hatem, 1993: 41–2). Neither do these authors shy away from an honest analysis of the implications for women of the rise of fundamentalist movements and the more profound Islamization of already Islamic countries.

At the other end are scholars whose theorization about women in the Middle East is more focused on locating Muslim women in history as social and political agents, not despite Islam but because of it (Afshar, 1994; L. Ahmed, 1992; Haddad and Smith, 1996; Haeri, 1995; Hassan, 1992; Javed, 1993; Marsot, 1996; Najmabadi, 1995; Tohidi, 1994; Yamani, 1996). To Muslim feminists among this group, only 'the ethical, egalitarian voice' in the Islamic message matters, not its 'legalistic voice'. Because even as Islam 'instituted a sexual hierarchy, it laid the ground, in its ethical voice, for the subversion of the hierarchy' (L. Ahmed, 1992: 238–9). The main argument of Riffat Hassan, for example, is that much of what Muslim women have experienced throughout the ages resulted from a deep-seated belief among Muslims about the differential rights of men and women. 'Muslims, in general, consider it a self-evident fact that women are not equal to men, who are "above" women or have a "degree of advantage" over them.' Not only have Muslim men 'arrogated to themselves the task of defining the ontological, theological, sociological and eschatological status of Muslim women', but they have prohibited the growth of scholarship on Islamic thought among women (Hassan, 1992: 41–3). Consequently, Muslim women are not aware that their Islamic rights have been violated by the male-centred societies in which they live. Hassan envisions a 'post-patriarchal' Islam which can secure women's legal and social rights. This will be possible through liberating Islamic Orthodox scripture from the yoke of male-centred, patriarchal interpretations of the Qur'an, the sunna, and hadith (traditions and sayings attributed to the prophet Muhammad), as laid down over the years. Women's urgent task is to deconstruct gendered Islamic discourses, and to challenge the ulamas' monolithic interpretational power. On this account, more women-friendly interpretations will eventually lead to favourable reforms in Islamic legal traditions and practices in ways more suited to these societies than those rooted in the strident, individualistic feminist advocacy of the West.

Others among this group, concerned primarily, perhaps, with challenging the racist and demonizing perceptions of Islam and its eternally gender-oppressive character, come close to denying the overpowering influence of religious practices and traditions alto-gether. Very few accept the Islamic framework in toto, as, for example, El Guindi (1996), El-Nimr (1996), Azzam (1996) and Fakhro (1996) do. Few, in conscience, can recommend it as a superior socio-legal system for protecting women's rights, viewing other perspectives as damaging to women's security or dignity, and advise their sisters to see the light and to put more faith in the inherently liberatory character of Islam. But some among them seem to have suddenly discovered the Islamic path to women's emancipation as the only viable, home-grown and culturally appropriate alternative to femi-nism, Marxism and the liberal humanist project. An increasing number of them are secular women who have turned to the Islamic framework as an indigenous, culturally accessible alternative to the West's feminist doctrine and practice.

Indeed, however brilliant some of these studies, very often they slip into a defensive, refractory position vis-à-vis Islam and its treat-ment of women. In their desire to respect the right of the previously silenced and misrepresented Muslim woman to speak for herself

and to smash the imagery of her as victimized, mute and domesticated, these writings present an enviably rosy picture of women's
lives in Islamic societies with little correspondence to reality. As an
alternative to the older, more passive image, a new notion of Muslim
women is constructed which is as essentializing and as irrelevant to
the realities of the overwhelming majority of women in these
countries as it was in typical Orientalist writings. If, in the past,
Muslim women could not be seen as anything but victims of male
aggression, now they are represented as independent-minded,
gender-conscious citizens who participate in the social and political
life of their societies; have adopted the veil as a brave act of defiance
against the social corruption of a Western-oriented market economy
and against consumerism (Abu-Odeh, 1992); and are challenging
the *ulamas'* hegemonic power over the interpretation of the sacred
texts (Najmabadi, 1995). A return to Islam, we are advised, will
guarantee women's rights in marriage and family matters and in the
management of their own money (Haddad, 1994). Already such
changes have made women protagonists in their own life dramas
(Haeri, 1995). Muslim women, therefore, represent an indigenous
non-Westoxicated model of liberated women to all women in these
societies (Tohidi, 1994).

Seen in this context, female seclusion, sex segregation and the
Islamic veil, traditional or revived, should not be seen as symbols
of male control over female sexuality and moral conduct, emblematic of the objectification of women. They should not be regarded
as instruments to limit women's activities or to punish women for
their imagined, omnipresent and active sexuality. Instead, we should
see the Islamic veil as a tool of female empowerment. Indeed, post-
coloniality requires that we see Islamic dress, so mystified and
misunderstood in the West, simply as clothing that may be worn to
beautify the wearer, much in the same way as Western women are
free to wear make-up (Hoodfar, 1993) – a 'creative alternative' developed by women to increase their participation in public spaces
or an anti-consumerist claim for women's right to modesty, to
control of their own bodies, to sexual space and moral privacy (El
Guindi, 1996: 161). We should see the veil, therefore, as a democratic
practice which erases class origins, giving women a greater degree

of social mobility while preserving their native culture and signalling a determination to move forward to modernity (L. Ahmed,
1992: 225). For young women it also serves as a remedy for discomfort in their daily lives, protecting them against sexual harass-
ment (Abu Odeh, 1992: 30–2).

At best, these accounts are privileged snapshots from the much
larger, often troubled, and, undoubtedly, multidimensional life drama
of women in Islamic societies, made particularly strenuous in societies where fundamentalism is not merely an ideology urged in
opposition but a clearly declared and forcefully implemented policy
of the state. Certainly, I agree with the authors that to better understand the situation of women in Islamic societies we should look to
their personal experiences and hear their own voices. It is also true
that many women for various reasons have been able to use the veil
to break down certain barriers to their participation in public spaces
in Islamic societies which were closed to them previously. My
concern, however, is that in the name of validating women's 'self-
perceptions' and 'hearing women's own voices', only the voices of
particular groups of women are heard and that then these voices are
broadcast as the unanimous expression of 'women in Islamic societies'. Worse still, the conditions of these women and the practical,
legitimate reasons behind their voices do not excite any further or
more thorough examination.

## The Veil as a Tool of Empowerment?

Many arguments made in support of *hejab* as a tool of women's
empowerment suffer from a myopic view of the practice. To use a
popular postmodern term, let us *deconstruct* the veil argument. But
we will explore the issue by using an 'old-fashioned' holistic
approach which considers objective conditions, together with experi-
ential, discursive and anecdotal materials. We begin with the presumed choice of *hejab* by women. In the writings which view the
veil as a tool of empowerment, the element of choice is taken for
granted, while, more often than not, the element of coercion, be it
in the form of using brutal force or intimidation, or social, cultural
and political pressure, is not even mentioned. The facts from differ-

ent Islamic societies, however suggest that this latter element is considerable.

In Iran, for example, *hejab* still represents one of the country's torments, twenty years after the 1979 Revolution. Legislation and government rulings make veiling mandatory. Improperly veiled (*bad-hejab*) women are subjected to harsh legal and extra-legal punishment. How can these realities be reconciled with ideas of the veil as a conscious and well-considered choice by 'Muslim women' designed to facilitate entry to previously barred public space? In Algeria, the 'choice' for women is between wearing a veil or not staying alive (Bennoune, 1995: 187). In Sudan, after Numeiri's downfall in 1989, imposition of the Islamic dress code was among the first revolutionary acts of the fundamentalist military junta. Sudanese professional women are harassed and questioned by the regime and self-appointed 'moral guards' about their presence in public and their relationships to the men seen in their company (Hale, 1996: 88–91, 111, 192). Where fundamentalists are still in the opposition, we see other forms of coercion to impose the veil. In the West Bank and Gaza Strip attempts by Hamas to force women to wear headscarves are backed by intimidation and threats. Women who refuse are presented as collaborators with the Israelis (Glavanis-Grantham, 1995). In liberated Iraq, or Kurdistan, the two rival Kurdish factions, to appease the Islamic Republic of Iran, have tried to impose *hejab* on Kurdish women by issuing orders. In Jordan, where Islamic practices are still being negotiated, the campaign to remodel women is pursued through what Lisa Taraki calls 'the carrot-and-stick approach'. A deluge of material on *hejab* tries to convince women 'of the virtues of the *hejab* and the danger of mixing with men'. Women 'missionaries' visit homes or give sermons at mosques warning women 'of the fires of hell, juxtaposing images of [the] suffering errant against those of women happy, content, and protected under the Islamic way of life' (Taraki, 1996: 147). Some Jordanian women, perhaps, are influenced by the fundamentalists' arguments and have adopted *hejab*, either for political or for spiritual reasons. But we must give equal weight to the experiences of larger sections of the female population who either refuse to wear *hejab* altogether, or do so for very practical reasons – to avoid men's aggressive sexual comments or touching in the streets (Abu Odeh, 1992), or to find employment, for example, in institutions like the Islamic Hospital in Amman which requires the Islamic dress code and insists on a policy of sexual segregation (Taraki, 1996).

In Egypt, the revived veil is linked to the failure of over a century of capitalist modernization to secure palpable improvements in women's lives or change cultural and religious patriarchal values and practices. After a century of modernization driven by the West, the choice for many remains between the security and protection that the Islamists promise and the cruel exploitation of a corrupt and mismanaged market economy. In other words, it is the crisis of Third World-style modernization that defines women's choices, not the spiritual and ideological attraction of Islam and the veil. Studying Cairo's newly veiled lower-middle-class women, Arlene Macleod found that for some the veil represented a turning back to a more authentic way of life. The majority, however, saw the new fashion as a way to get married; and even these women were sharply critical of the beliefs and actions of Islamic groups, identifying these militants as 'bad Muslims', even 'criminals' (Macleod, 1991: 109–13). In fact, some upper- and middle-class women, Nawal El Saadawi tells us, 'import their veils from the West; some of them do not know their indigenous language and culture' (El Saadawi, 1997: 96). As Hala Shukrallah has argued, Egyptian Muslim women and Christians have been made the objects of concerted cultural representations constructing them in relation to Western domination. In the Islamists' pretended reconstruction of the 'true community', women are pushed to assume the role of a symbolic antithesis to modernism and the West. Since women are at the heart of the community, any non-conformity makes them the target of fierce attack (Shukrallah, 1994: 24–5).

Coercion and intimidation work in dangerous and horrifying ways in both Jordan and Egypt. In both countries, the charge of apostasy (kofr) – a crime punishable by death in Islamic societies – is used to intimidate political opponents and to silence secular forces, women included. In Egypt, for example, a group of Islamist lawyers filed a suit in 1993 to divorce a Cairo professor from his wife, against the couple's wishes and even without their knowledge, on the grounds that he was a *kafar*, or atheist[3] (Colla, 1993). During her election campaign in the early 1980s charges of apostasy were also used against Toujan al-Faisal, the Jordanian female journalist and first woman elected to Jordan's parliament. Her crime? She has criticized the Islamists who use religion to terrorize people and she used Islamic law to defend women's rights. She threatened the Islamists in their own domain. 'They wanted to make an example of her and to intimidate those who held opinions different from their own' (Gallagher, 1995: 216).

The notion that *hejab* fights consumerism and erases class distinctions is also wishful thinking at best. Class divisions in fact are deepening among women in the Middle East and North Africa. Should we believe that Islamic societies are egalitarian and classless, somehow untouched by the global market economy? Would it not be rather simplistic to think that a piece of cloth can erase class divisions and class privileges among women? The reality is quite different. Taraki tells us that in Jordan, for example, hiding under the *jilibah* are clothes which are highly diverse, influenced by − if not replicas of − Western styles. In Iran well-to-do women hide bold European fashions under the *chador*. It is a known fact that the ayatollahs' wives and daughters and *nouveau-riche* mullahs are regular customers in exclusive boutiques selling brand-name imported clothing which other middle-class women cannot afford to buy. Even the material used for the *chador* itself varies considerably, signalling clear differences in class and wealth.

Also highly debatable is the idea that the veil can serve as a protective shield granting women security from men's sexual advances. Veiling and the strict Islamic code for enforcing public morality have never proved sufficient to protect women against rape by their Muslim 'brothers'. The protection was not there for Bangladeshi women during the war of partition. Neither was the protection on hand for Iranian and Kuwaiti women during the Iran–Iraq and Persian Gulf wars. The Islamic code did not help women in Afghanistan and in Algeria; in fact, the threat to them increased during two decades of civil war when religious issues were brought to the fore and political conflict raged between fundamentalists and the state. As Nazih Ayubi has argued, it may be that sexually repressed Muslim men find aggression against women, including female relatives, to be the only outlet available for the release of their frustrations (Ayubi, 1995).

That the obsession with sex, women and the human body is so strong that its borders on the pathological is even acknowledged by some Islamist writers. They admit that the veil and segregation and 'turning the eye away' are not the solution, because 'the larger the veil, the greater the desire to recognize what it hides!' (Hasan Hanafi cited in Ayubi, 1995: 91). This is given credence by the growth of sex tourism in Egypt (El-Gawhary, 1995) and the alarming increase in Iran of sexual crime, including rapes and horrifying murders of women.[4] As Nawal El Saadawi remarks, women in Islamic societies are caught between the globalized image of femininity or female beauty as a commodity in the West and the Islamic notion of femininity 'protected' by men and hidden behind the veil. In fact, 'veiling and nakedness are two sides of the same coin. Both mean that women are bodies without a mind and should be covered or uncovered in order to suit national or international capitalist interests' (El Saadawi, 1997: 138–40).

On close examination, it seems justifications of the veil or other Islamic practices, despite their radical appearance, are factually inaccurate and politically quite conservative. Indeed, many of the writings on women and Islam discuss specific practices without any meaningful references to Islamic fundamentalism, one of the most potent ideological, political and philosophical challenges of our time to feminism and the feminist concept of women's individual autonomy and the right to choose. Drawn to the justified pleas for greater tolerance for diasporic Muslim communities – the main targets of racist Islamophobia in the West – some writers, knowingly or unknowingly, find themselves making an appeal for more tolerance as well of the brutal Islamist states; they call attention to the 'brighter sides' for women of Islamification, seeking acceptance of degrading practices as simply a 'different way of life'.[5] In the process, they soften the harsh edges of fundamentalism; they help validate the image that fundamentalists transmit of Muslim women as emblematic of cultural revival, integrity and authenticity in Islamic societies. They endorse, in effect, the fundamentalists' solutions to crisis of modernity and of modernization.

If the aim is to confront the essentialized images of Muslims and to interrogate the colonial reduction of women's identity to its Islamic 'essence,' then, by all means, we should start by validating women's actual experience, bringing out positive and life-affirming aspects of indigenous cultural practices and women's local responses. But in the postmodern climate, the interrogation often stops there. These writers very often privilege the discourses of specific groups of women, those of the 'authentic', empowered 'Muslim' women, erasing the diversity of women's experiences along lines which cut across class, ethnicity, ideology and politics in North Africa and the Middle East.

In sum, I present two arguments. First, that in the post-colonial, anti-Orientalist scholarship on Islam and gender what we are increasingly confronted with is a convergence of the seemingly radical, anti-representational view with a fundamentalist conservatism. Second, that this convergence represents a style of thought shaped by postmodern relativism, which dominates the European and, particularly, the North American academy – as a style benchmarked by an uncritical pursuit of the culturally exotic and the untouched. At philosophical and political levels there is a profound failure to draw a clear distinction between the position of fundamentalists and that of a large number of anti-representational post-colonial feminists. At a tremendous cost to women in the Islamic world, concepts of universality, equality, modernity and human rights are lost, as the differences between the vocabulary and the stance of these two positions become less visible.

## Notes

1. For two exceptionally rigorous critiques of *Orientalism*, see Ahmad (1992) and Al-Azm (1981).

2. For a very enlightening account of the racialized war metaphors, see De Awis (1991) and Norton (1991).

3. In August 1996, the Court of Cassation, Egypt's highest court, upheld the ruling of a lower court that Professor Nasr Hamed Abu Zeid must divorce his wife because he denounced Islam. See *Guardian Weekly*, 18 August 1996.

4. In 1997 two cases of sexual assault and murder shocked Tehran. In one case, nine girls and young women were murdered after being raped

(*Iran Farda*, No. 36, 1997: 5). In another case, a young man had raped over thirty women by hiding in a hairdressing salon he had established for the purpose (*Iran Star*, 7 December 1997: 24).

5. This trend is gaining ground, particularly among Iranian feminist scholars in the West. In many of these writings, rosy pictures are drawn of the situation of women in Iran which work to sanitize the Islamization policies of the Islamic state (Afshar, 1994; Hoodfar, 1993; Mir-Hoseinin, 1996; Ramazani, 1993; Tohidi, 1994).

# Chapter 3

# Postmodern Relativism and the Politics of Cultural Difference

Nostalgic populism and identity politics are intellectual tendencies which smother common sense and repress sound political judgement. I want to argue that nostalgia, or 'the disease of melancholic scholars', as Bryan Turner would have it, is the leading motif of the recent exuberant discussion of Muslim women's gender activism which represents 'Muslim women' as empowered, militant and dignified citizens with a firmly integrated sense of self. Which is to say the Orientalists' construction of shimmering illusory images of Oriental Muslim women is now confronted by turning the genre on its head.

Racism and Islamophobia in the West, as I argued earlier, nurture and sustain such positions. This enthusiastic tendency might also originate from what the anthropologist Robert Redfield identified years ago as 'the lower moral expectation' applied to the 'simpler societies'. We are less critical of them, he wrote, because 'we do not expect them to protect freedom of thought the same as we do', and 'we do not fault them for subjugation and repression the way that we do in respect to Russia or to the United States' (Redfield cited in Hatch, 1983: 107). More recently Henry Munson Jr identified the trend as 'the Lawrence of academia syndrome'. This condition, he wrote:

> leads Western scholars to leap to the defense of any and all aspects of the societies they study, especially third-world societies, even if this means defending conduct they would never tolerate in their own country

and even if it means ignoring or criticizing intellectuals from the societies they study who condemn the very things they defend. (Munson, 1996: 102–3)

Whatever its roots, this intellectual trend might prove too costly for the individuals or societies studied. The newly manufactured image of strong Muslim women in active negotiation with a Muslim male elite might produce contradictory consequences. It might ornament gender experience under Islamic fundamentalism and mystify the consequences of non-compliance for women who do not share the beliefs of their Muslim sisters. I want to argue, however, that this trend gets its theoretical inspiration, particularly, from postmodernist relativism, which, for better or worse, has emerged as a fascinating antidote to the Eurocentric totalizing metatheories and the universalism of liberal pluralism, Marxism and feminism.

## The Postmodern Frame

An intellectual trend, a fashion of thought and language, postmodernist subversion and scepticism offers a seduction we can hardly resist. Often used 'loosely' as an open-ended, self-explanatory umbrella term, postmodernism means a variety of things to different people. Its 'popular' usage does not necessarily reflect all its complex philosophical attributes. Here, I will engage only with aspects of the postmodern perspective which are relevant to theorization about women in Islamic societies. Features of the postmodern frame which are relevant to our specific study here can be outlined in the following terms:

- the disenchantment with the foundation of modern social thought, with Western modernity, and the demystification of scientific objectivity and objective knowledge;
- the emphasis on narratives and the rejection of metanarratives and grand theories;
- suspicion of classical notions of reason, truth, universal progress, and the rejection of the idea of the existence of a hidden essential meaning and direction in history, with the emphasis, instead, on discontinuity, difference and the celebration of the 'local';

- the concern over representations of the 'Other', both imagined and real, and over processes of marginalization of Others;
- an absorption with language and the study of discourse as ways of thinking and speaking which reflect the distribution of power in society;
- an engagement with questions of sexuality as a historical construct and with sexual diversity and difference;
- a preoccupation with identity and with the notion of identity as a choice not a destiny;
- a mistrust of power;
- an awareness that the way things are and are done is not the only way and that all beliefs and knowledge are cultural constructs, and hence contingent and conversable.

Not surprisingly, the reaction of academics to postmodernism has been quite diverse. For some writers, the postmodern approach assists those constructed as 'Other' in reclaiming their own histories and their own voice (Giroux, 1994: 24); it has taught us 'to play subversive games with traditional codes' (Tijssen, 1991: 161). Postmodernism, by 'announcing de-centering of the subject, the end of metanarratives (including Marxism), the interlocking of knowledge and power, and the substitution of politics of difference for a millennial liberationist politics, offers a potentially useful vantage point from which to rethink theory and politics in at least some Western nations' (Nicholson and Seidman, 1995: 7–8).

At the other end, however, are those who are critical of the postmodern perspective because it undermines the foundation of political democracy (Habermas, 1993). The postmodern frame has also been criticized for its rejection of Marxism, and for normalizing capitalist contradictions under the category of difference (Ebert, 1996: 150–1); for its ethnocentrism and for 'its failure to grasp the profound significance of imperialism, colonialism and their associated racism as constitutive of modernity' (Rattansi and Westwood, 1994: 28–9). While postmodern thinking is given credit for putting questions of sexuality, gender and ethnicity firmly on the political agenda, it is criticized for its disregard for class structure and material conditions (Eagleton, 1996: 22).

For all this, the postmodern view, stripped of its exaggerated arcane language, can be of help in opening new lines of inquiry or in breaking through the confines of the structuralist and culturalist impasse. Working within the Marxist canon, for example, postmodern thinking can help us go beyond the sterile opposition of 'determining' base and 'determined' superstructure, emphasizing the *interaction* of political and economic struggle and cultural forms, and doing away with the notion that political and economic structures may 'prefigure' or 'predict' the ways in which ideas are lived.[1]

As mentioned earlier, however, my concern here is less with postmodernism as a slippery epistemological stance and more with its effects on our political climate and mood – its well-advertised but fictitious radicalism, which rapidly dissolves into a celebration of cultural difference, its privileging of the 'local' (as against 'master narratives' emphasizing universal rights), and, in consequence, its curious affinity with the most reactionary ideas of Islamic fundamentalism. For the two share a common ground – an unremitting hostility to the social, cultural and political processes of change and knowledge and rationality, originating in the West, known as modernity. The acceptance of the idea of the cultural specificity of the morals and manners of society by postmodernism has quickly turned into relativism and the view that there is no such thing as the validity of truth and rationality, no commitment to power of reason or to 'principled intellectual inquiry', because 'discourses are incommensurable and cannot be compared or judged against one another' (McLennan, 1996: 645–7).

The most powerful impact of postmodernism comes from its critique of the Enlightenment. As a broad cultural and social movement, the Enlightenment represented an attempt to free humanity from the grip of medieval religion and metaphysics. In Europe, it provoked a foundation for modern social and political institutions; it offered intellectual grounds for notions of individual rights and secular citizenship. Despite disagreements among postmodernists, starting with Nietzsche, all agree that the Enlightenment project was a spectacular failure. Nietzsche, as the first deconstructionist, pronounces on the West's decay in *Thus Spoke Zarathustra*, which, as Stanley Rosen points out, is a critique of Europe from the standpoint of an

Oriental, an outsider. In *Zarathustra*, a Persian prophet annihilates the West's claims to civilization from a higher perspective; but Nietzsche's nihilism is merely the first stage of a revolutionary project which must first destroy and then create (Rosen, 1995: 7–8). Revisiting the West's Eurocentric and often power-serving notions of truth, reason and progress – its all but scriptural faith in the emancipatory power of science and of scientific truth – postmodernists challenge all manner of totalizing metatheories and universalism. They draw our attention to the deeply embedded cultural assumptions behind 'universal reason' – the asserted universality of social and historical progress and the unidirectionality of humanity's intellectual and moral striving. Questioning the transhistorical claims of the Enlightenment vision, postmodernists argue that various cultures move in different directions and proceed at different speeds.

Supporting this critique are pluralistic notions of morality and knowledge. On this view, there is no single, superior way of knowing and being; our moral and ethical judgements are rooted in biased standards – and those who set standards have the backing of structures and relations which work to disempower anyone who dares to disagree. Indeed, human needs are diverse. What appears as desirable to one culture is useless or even destructive for another. Human societies, for better or worse, proceed with their own rhythm towards their own goals.

## Rethinking Modernity in the Middle East?

Anti-modernism and anti-universalism fascinate intellectuals committed to an anti-representational scholarship. But I want to argue that one runs grave risks in rejecting modernity in its totality when discussing social and political developments and gender relations in Islamic societies. There is no question that generally too much faith has been placed on the liberating force of modernization, exemplified in economic growth and technological advance. Growth has been taken, incautiously, as the embodiment of rationality and progress. There is no question that too little attention has been paid to what constitutes modernization – who profits from it, and at what costs. But to reject modernization and modernity as irrelevant and

undesirable projects for Islamic societies opens the door to a disastrous politics.

To start, we need to differentiate between modernity and modernization. 'Modernization' in the Middle East, as in other parts of the
so-called 'Third World', has meant only economic growth, capital
accumulation and industrialization under the auspices of multinational corporations, led by an authoritarian elite and serving the
interests of a privileged minority. 'Modernity', however, implies a
broad totality including political and cultural as well as economic
dimensions. Historically, in Europe, modernity included or eventually
led to social justice, political democracy, secularism and, perhaps
most importantly, state accountability and the rule of law. Legal
advance, it was recognized, was needed to protect individual autonomy and basic human rights. This project, or at least elements
of it, have been achieved in the West. Legal rights, including women's
rights, are enforced by the state.

Using these criteria, one can perhaps say that modernity has not
even begun in the Islamic world. There, instead, we witness a gro-
tesque modernization without modernism and without modernity,
a lopsided change, which alters aspects of the urban economy but
without fundamentally transforming social and political structures
or relations and forms of cultural expression. In these societies, a
huge gap opens (or widens) between a privileged minority and a
majority which remains virtually untouched by growth, or which
suffers from it. This absurd and pathetic result explains the reaction
to modernization by large sections of the population in the Middle
East and North Africa and hence their call for an alternative – an
alternative that has given rise, in this part of the world, to religious
fundamentalisms. Now, if modernity in its full sense has not even
started in the Islamic world, how can we even understand the
rejectionist position taken by postmodernists? Is rejection *tout court*
a viable liberatory theoretical project for the Middle East?

If we give in to despair, then the postmodernists' arguments
about the failed promises of modernity are quite persuasive. Indeed,
one need not wonder about the fascination with postmodernism
which has captured the West. It may stem from a collapse of hope
in the contemporary world; it may reflect a capitulation, in Eric

Hobsbawm's words, to a situation where no effective limits on behaviour any longer exist, and we seem to be sliding down the slope to barbarism (Hobsbawm, 1994). Thus, far from marching in the direction of 'universal reason' and 'self-realization', humanity seems to have lost its sense of direction. Seen in this light, post-modernism is a response to the political, socio-cultural and economic crises of the last decades. Economic exploitation; homelessness and poverty; environmental destruction; race riots and racialized injustice; sexual abuse and gendered violence; incompetent and corrupt state management; the incapacity of sophisticated scientific medicine to cure horrifying diseases; religious fundamentalism of the most atavistic sort; ethnic conflicts ripening into full-fledged, bloody wars – all these serve as symptoms, exposing the fragility of Enlightenment progress, the profound failure to share the benefits of scientific advance, secularism, the nation-state, democracy, legal equity, the rule of law, individual autonomy and freedom. They display the huge gap between the promises offered by modernity and the brutality and horror which take place under its banner. Should we be surprised if this leads to a deep insecurity and confusion prompting many to seek a return to religion? And we find that rush to religious consolation not only among ordinary citizens but even among the most privileged elite – corporate executives, bank managers, and businessmen and -women, who, we are told, have turned, for example, to lunch-break Bible-study groups and noon-hour communion services which flourish in business districts from Bay Street in Toronto to Halifax and Vancouver.[2]

When the craze for economic rationality, dominating every aspect of social life (what George Ritzer [1992] has called the 'McDonald-ization of society'), appears to have consumed our ability to make reasoned choices, and the projects of liberalism, Marxism and feminism each seem inadequate to cope with the West's 'crisis of identity', postmodernism presents itself as a seductive alternative, a 'local' escape. But intellectuals in the Middle East need to look at such proposals in the context of their own situation. Postmodernism remains a privilege for those who have enjoyed the benefits of modernity. It can remain a 'celebration of the pre-modernity of others', as Al-Azmeh would put it. It remains doubtful whether projects rejecting modernity can be helpful in areas which have not yet drawn the benefits of a stable political existence, democratic means of choice or the rule of law.

It is important to note that most critics of modernity regard the 'modern' as a two-sided historical process. That is to say that post-modernists still use Western modernity to criticize its foundation and to set themselves against the Enlightenment; they are both inside and outside of modernity, as Ali Rattansi notes. That is, they step back, or out, and look in, 'while still having one foot and eye, so to speak, inside modernity' (Rattansi and Westwood, 1994: 19). A complex set of changes in Europe dissolved premodern forms of domination, but created new forms of domination. Dialectical social critics, like Habermas, while criticizing problematic features of modern societies, favour the preservation of the 'emancipatory impulse' of the Enlightenment. Therefore, Habermas asks, instead of 'giving up modernity and its project as a lost cause', why don't we 'learn from the mistakes of those extravagant programs which have tried to negate modernity' (Habermas, 1993: 106)? As Nancy Fraser argues, even the position of Foucault, one of the most influential postmodern fathers, is highly ambiguous vis-à-vis the political ideas of the Enlightenment. Does he, for example, 'aspire to a total break with the longstanding Western tradition of emancipation via rational reflection?' Does he reject the project of bringing the 'background practices and institutions that structure the possibilities of social life' under the conscious collective control of human beings? Does he reject modernity in toto, or only one component of it, namely humanism (Fraser, 1994: 186–7).

To reject modernity in the Middle East without offering a more humane and egalitarian alternative is to validate fundamentalism, celebrating its non-Western, non-Eurocentric, home-grown, culturally harmonious values as the only hope appropriate for the Islamic world. Middle Eastern intellectuals must decide whether modernism is an alien and alienating idea for the Islamic world, or whether, as Al-Azmeh argues, it provides the germ of a universal civilization that, 'from mercantile beginnings, came utterly to transform the economies, societies, polities, and cultures of the world, and to reconstitute the non-European world in terms of actually existing historical breaks' (Al-Azmeh, 1993: 21). Consider, for example, the Sufis, who rejected the idea of blind submission, or the Falasifa, who speculated on the philosophical foundations of the world and raised the question of the place of reason and personal opinion. As Fatima Mernissi remarks, these two movements did exactly what Western philosophers of the Enlightenment did. They 'raised the same issues that we are today told are imports from the West' (Mernissi, 1992: 20–1).

All this comes down to the question as to what is the most practical way to look at the project of modernity in the Middle East today? Is it to respond to the fundamentalists' advances through distancing ourselves from the Western philosophical and intellectual frameworks which promised emancipation and to seek something within these own countries' histories which is internally rooted? Is it to 'unearth' modernist ideas which have native roots, and to identify and trace the histories of early modernizing efforts within the Islamic world which were defeated? Or is it to dig deeper, and explain the causes of the defeats which indigenous reform movements and ideas suffered when attempts were made to bring elements of 'modernity' (whatever their provenance) to the Islamic world?

Historian Homa Nateq's research on early-nineteenth-century Iran, for example, reveals a short-lived period in the country's history when rational ideas and an ideological commitment to 'rationalism' dominated the Iranian polity. Under the Sufi king Muhammad Shah (and his Sufi teacher, Mirza Aghasi, as Prime Minister), Iran saw a brief but instructive period of progress and toleration, and respect for non-Muslims' rights. This period (1834–48), identified by Nateq as Iran's abbreviated 'enlightenment' (*Rowshangari*), was marked by radical developments such as the recognition of equal rights for Muslims, Jews and Christians; the abolition (by royal decree) of torture and the death penalty; and the establishment of the first girls' schools. In the cultural-religious crisis which engulfed the country after its defeat in 1826 by Russia, Iran was caught up in self-doubt and self-criticism, and a need was felt to reconsider, or revisit, certain basic values. Nateq describes how blame for the military defeats and Iran's general backwardness was assigned to the influence of the Islamic clergy. For centuries, the clerics blocked

new ideas and practices, stifling all thought outside the prescriptions of the *Shari'a*. A movement was begun to remove the Muslim
clergy from political power and to weaken their influence in the
larger community, to replace age-old religious superstitions and
archaic institutions with more tolerant civic traditions (urf) and
modern social values.

But reforms were too short-lived for the changes to be institu-
tionalized. When Muhammad Shah died, Mirza Aghasi was banished,
and the old ways returned. The Iranian clergy regained its power.
The Babis, an anti-clerical and anti-feudal reform movement that
had previously escaped persecution, were now made subject to mass
arrest. Seyyed Mohammed Ali Bab, their leader, was executed. Freedom of religion was annulled, and the Jews persecuted. The death
penalty returned, including women's stoning to death on charges of
adultery. The clergy reclaimed its monopoly over Islam as the sole
legitimate basis for intellectual and philosophical thought. How do
we account for the fragility of Iran's 'enlightenment'? In commenting
on the episode and the reverses which followed, Nateq emphasizes
that 'Muslims cannot place all the blame at the door of colonialism
and imperialism.' Indeed, in many ways,

> we have been our own enemy. Cultural, social and political advance-
> ment cannot be achieved through religious means.... Whenever Muslims
> fail to provide good explanations and analysis, they try to dig up rotten
> past ideas: we have been this and we have been that. We introduced this
> or that knowledge to the world. We gave the world this or that scientist....
> We cannot blame someone else for our weaknesses, thoughtlessness and
> faults. (Nateq, 1990: 250–1)

The point is that if Middle Eastern intellectuals wish to join in
a critique of 'modernity', they will need to clarify for themselves
what alternative exists for the Islamic world. Blessed by democratic
social, political and cultural institutions, Western intellectuals may
be able to take a sharp look at rationality, humanism, universalism
and modernity. Protected as they are, they will not come to harm
if they entertain fantasies about communal bonding, the exotic, the
small and local, or romanticize premodern practices and institutions, harbouring hopes in them for authentic cultural practices
which would respond to human spiritual needs. It was populist

politics, perhaps, this excitement with the 'authentic' and 'anti-modern', which made Michel Foucault stir in fascination at the Islamic movement in Iran, seeing the Islamic veil as a political protest against the Shah's modernization project. Foucault was drawn, as well, to Khomeini and his followers, who – in their anti-modernist movement (he thought) – were looking for something that the French had forgotten: a 'political spirituality' (Eribon, 1991: 286). But the angry response at the time of an anonymous Iranian woman in *Le Nouvel Observateur* to Foucault's ill-founded hopes was quite justified. 'The Western left', she wrote, 'is sufficiently lacking in humanism to find Islam desirable – for others.' She expected 'the liberal left in the West to know what an iron mantle Islamic law is capable of becoming'. And she went on to say that the left 'should not let itself be seduced by a remedy that is worse, perhaps, than the illness'. Eribon notes that Foucault later recognized his great mistake.

In supporting the rights of minority cultures and indigenous traditions, we should ask ourselves: do we know with any precision *whose cultures* and *whose rights* to self-expression we are supporting? What are the social and political contexts and power relations behind particular forms of cultural expression? Who has assumed the authority for cultural representation in particular cases, and why? In raising these questions, it is of the utmost importance to remember that culture and 'cultural difference' are not transhistorical entities. Neither are they homogeneous. Each culture is criss-crossed by internal class, religious, ethnic and regional divisions. Cultures do not have a life of their own, unaffected by social, economic and political change, stressful internal and external forces, and highly differentiated structures of power and disempowerment. As Barrington Moore Jr remarks, 'cultures and value systems are maintained and transmitted with much suffering and pain. Very often, to get humans to behave in specific ways, they must be punched, bullied, sent to jail, thrown into concentration camps, cajoled, bribed, made into heroes, encouraged to read newspapers, stood up against a wall and shot' (Moore, 1967: 487).

Moreover, one should be cautious in theorizing about 'alternative' social and political movements, particularly when events and discourses taking shape in Islamic societies are analysed in isolation from their specific national and regional context. To avoid mystification, we need to take into account the particular setting for such events and not to be intimidated by charges that this insistence constitutes a metanarrativist intrusion. Consider, for example, the debates over clitoridectomy in France, where these surgeries are practised among migrant North African communities. To discourage the practice, performers of clitoridectomy and the parents of the victims – girls aged four, five or seven years – were legitimately brought to trial to discourage the practice. However, cultural relativists opposed the legal action for its interference in the intimacy of families (Bronwyne, 1994). Indeed, a prominent French academic and a committed supporter of 'respect for the customs of cultural minorities', Raymond Verdier, among others, argued that mutilation is a relative notion, determined by cultural conditioning, and that clitoridectomy is 'an act of social incorporation into a group of women', insisting that 'a good number of accused parents see in it a Muslim custom.' Verdier even claimed that African women approached clitoridectomy with 'joyful acceptance', suggesting that since the practice is so important culturally, African women suffer less from it than a white woman would. The Movement pour la Defense des droits de la Femme Noire in France protested this blatantly racist argument. For in the name of cultural tolerance, it implied that the pain of torture and injury is different for European and non-European people and that it perceives just one universal and monolithic 'African culture' (Bronwyne, 1994: 954–6).

The position of Verdier and other pro-diversity academics is reminiscent of British magistrates' reports on sati (the practice of burning widows alive) in colonial India. The colonial administration decided to regulate sati rather than abolish it, despite the long struggle of Indian intellectuals against the custom. Here, again, the reports represented the widow, who was about to be burned alive, as marching into the flames with contentment and joy, and of her own free will – obscuring the hidden coercion exercised by the surviving relatives who desired to be rid of the financial burden of supporting the widow and the widow's legal right over the family estate (Mati, 1990: 88–126).

Rather than getting defensive or apologetic about their rejection of fundamentalism or Western intervention in the region, secular Middle Eastern scholars need to make clear why they stand opposed to both. To oppose Western imperialistic interests in Islamic states, challenging Western attempts to present Islam as the 'new danger' in a 'post-communist' era, should not mean supporting the fundamentalists' self-serving, anti-Western perspectives in the name of anti-imperialism; nor does criticism, however sharp, of the manifold failures of Western 'modernity' or the shortcomings of 'modernization' in the East require celebration of the 'primitive' and 'local' among socio-economic and cultural structures and institutions.

Islamic societies cannot advance by relying on pre-industrial cultural values and ideas. As Tibi argues, rather than complaining of 'Europe' or of European historical notions of 'enlightenment' and 'democracy', we would do better to focus our attention on contemporary European (and North American) powers which proclaim (but only in words) the imminent 'Europeanization' of the non-Western world, while doing everything they can to prevent it in deeds. If 'modernization' is to have real substance in the Third World, it must not consist, merely, of a transformation in norms but include, instead, industrialization and a profound democratization (Tibi, 1988: 28). Furthermore, even if the Enlightenment's modernizing impulse were rooted, originally, in European traditions, the wish for 'modernity', shared social responsibility and individual rights can no longer be regarded as something peculiarly European: 'these are now parts of universal, human, demands, and no longer can be restricted to specific cultures or to the rich states' (Tibi, 1988: 18). For Middle Eastern intellectuals, 'the struggle between secular modernism and Islamic revival is fundamentally a struggle about secular democracy, economic justice, and the liberation of women'; ultimately a claim to replace existing society with a modern, secular society (Sharabi, 1992: 137).

In such a context, the adoption of postmodernism's anti-universalist tenets is very risky, even politically irresponsible. Arguing that no universal standard exists for human progress and that societies proceed with 'different speeds' and in 'different ways' overlooks the crucial question of why the proposed standards did not work in

colonial and post-colonial countries. Can we imagine that the development of each of these different worlds has been totally independent?
Was one world's speedy development not directly contingent upon,
or, at least, costly to, the other world? Yes, colonialism and the slave
trade speeded up the West's industrial development, but what did
they do to Asia and Africa?

It is also politically problematic to use postmodernism's fragmented conceptual framework to select the countries for which
individual liberties and rights to self-determination, national identity and cultural authenticity are deemed appropriate. Such an approach quickly breeds indifference towards poor countries and
peoples outside the West. It suggests that suffering from poverty,
repression and violence is somehow endemic and 'natural', and need
not be a cause for worries in the West. Eventually, people in these
societies will solve their problems at 'their own pace and rhythm',
and we owe them the respect of letting this occur. Besides, the
meaning of 'suffering' and 'poverty' are themselves subjects of debate,
and have to be culturally defined, locally, before any global response
can legitimately be offered.

It should be clear that this convoluted understanding of cultural
difference is incompatible with a commitment to the defence of
human rights. Whatever their intent, arguments which assert the
right of different cultures to establish, define and exercise their own
standards, meanings and principles play directly into the hands of
political and economic elites, religious leaders and authoritarian
regimes, and, above all, fundamentalists, who argue, for their own
purposes, that the notion of human rights is 'culture-bound' and
Western, that international measures for human rights are imperialist
ploys. In the effort to show respect for cultural diversity, care should
be taken not to leave too much to the discretion of non-Western
states when their leaders object to 'Western' values. For often the
elite that raise 'culture' as a defence against external criticism have
no difficulty, themselves, in suppressing the cultures of their own
ethnic or religious or political minorities, suppressing customs ruth-
lessly when they are not convenient (Donnelly, 1989: 119). Authoritarian leaders in Islamic societies sometimes oppose what they
describe as 'Western' notions of individual rights in the name of

collective values or of the sanctified community of believers, the umma.
Their main concern, however, is somewhere else. They wish, first of
all, to insulate themselves from internal challenges and international
scrutiny. And they wish to continue with their open, sometimes
legally sanctioned, political, cultural, ethnic, religious and sexual
discriminatory practices directed against individuals and groups who
do not belong to dominant political and cultural interests.

Needless to say, the religious leaders who proclaim their opposition to imperialism and modernity have difficulty only with such
Western notions as political democracy, individual autonomy and
human rights, feeling that parliamentary institutions and democratic
state control are incompatible with the sacred quality of indigenous
cultures and traditions. They do not object, however, to adopting
the capitalist market economy of the West, albeit a disfigured and
inefficient version of it. Troubled only by institutions of democratic
insurgency, initiative or challenge, they do not object to accumulating
wealth or to using the stylish, technically sophisticated products
offered to them by the West.

The uncritical fascination with Western postmodernism can prove
a costly intellectual experiment for Middle Eastern intellectuals, who
inadvertently lend support to the most effectively cloaked repressive
movement in the region: Islamic fundamentalism.

## Notes

1. But this is merely to say that, sympathetically read, postmodernism
provides us with a language that reinstates the anti-determinist logic of
Marx's thought. See the useful formulation of cultural theory (sans postmodern ornaments, but with a compact summary of Gramsci's contribution) in Williams (1973).

2. The Globe and Mail, 9 February 1996.

# Chapter 4

# Islamic Fundamentalism and its Nostalgic Accomplice

Of all of today's theoretical, epistemological and methodological perspectives and 'isms', perhaps no two are as different in principle as postmodernism and religious fundamentalism. The fundamentalist belief in total, absolute 'truth' and its universal blueprint for human salvation are what postmodernists passionately dislike. Likewise, the unquestioning acceptance of *difference*, indeed, the celebration of the irreplaceable and unique, and the insistence on the multiplicity of signs, identities and texts – central to the postmodernist outlook – are what fundamentalists reject. Difference, uniqueness, claims to individual or group identities, rights to individual self-determination, and, particularly, the critique of sexual essentialism and the emphasis on sexual diversity are key points of contrast between postmodernism and fundamentalism. Indeed, intellectually to annihilate all that stays outside its closed, self-referenial cultural and moral frame is the first principle of the fundamentalists' political project. However, I want to argue that postmodern relativism, and elements of its frame of thought, bring it close to the fundamentalist conception of history and modernity as the product of Western capitalism. Consequently, it validates the fundamentalists' rejection of the social and moral ideas and standards associated with the project of modernity as the creation of a handful of Western nations, and thus not applicable to or suitable for Islamic societies. Among the elements of the postmodern frame which are glaringly concurrent with Islamic fundamentalist discourse and validate its political vision and practices are postmodernists' over-emphasis on cultural difference, plurality of knowledge, beliefs and social and moral standards; their dismissal of the faith in technology, science and reason and all-encompassing theories; as well as their fascination with community, ethnicity, otherness, transitional identity, local factors, 'local victories', popular culture and their search for social and cultural variety and new 'emancipatory narratives'. But I need to spend some time to clarify why I use the term 'fundamentalism' in this book.

## Islamic Fundamentalism Defined

It is rare for a scholarly piece on Islamic fundamentalism not to begin by defining the term and then pointing to its inadequacies.[1] To distance themselves from stereotypical analyses, authors use the term fundamentalism reluctantly and apologetically to describe new radical Islamic movements or to offer substitute terms for it such as 'revivalist', 'religious nationalists', 'Islamic radicals', 'Islamic populists' or 'Islamists' (Davis, 1984; Juergensmeyer, 1993; Nasr, 1997; Rahnema, 1994). These concerns may be justified given the fact that the term originated in the West in relation to Protestantism, and the fundamentalists do not use the term as a mark of their identity. How the two fundamentalisms can be equated is also not obvious. But for the reasons I outline below, I believe none of the substitutes suggested can properly define the new radical Islamic movements.[2] Besides, like Sadiq Al-Azm, I am not persuaded by the argument that we should not apply terms to identify people who would not accept and apply them to themselves. Pointedly, Al-Azm asks, 'would we ever be able to say that such and such a Middle Eastern ruler is a "brutal military dictator," considering that he never applies such words and descriptions either to himself or to his regime?' (Al-Azm, 1993–94 Part I: 95).

This reasoning can be extended by considering how we apply the term 'Islamic feminism', for example, to groups of women in the Middle East who try to challenge traditional Islamic discourses and legal traditions, demanding a just treatment of women. They never apply the term 'feminists' to themselves, or ever consider 'feminist ideas' as applicable to the Middle East. Indeed, these women use every opportunity to distance themselves from what they understand as feminist ideals and feminist politics and practices in the West. Still they are referred to as 'Islamic feminists' because of certain observable features in their discourses and activities.

In all this, as Marx reminds us in his analysis of the bourgeois revolutionaries of 1848, we should not allow ourselves to be deceived by the draperies with which political actors and intellectuals choose to wrap themselves, calling on departed spirits and the glories of the past – or on a wish, however generous, to 'soften' or erase the sharp edges of their acts – but, instead, we should look directly at what they actually say and do, and decide for ourselves the names for this behaviour that will make the best sense (Marx, 1973: 146–7). Indeed, 'our opinions of an individual' as Marx wrote, in another context, 'is never based on what he thinks of himself' (Marx, 1984: 390).

'Islamic revivalism' is not a new phenomenon. It dates back, at least, to Imam Muhammad Ghazali (1058–1111) (Rahnema, 1994). Not all revivalists are fundamentalists, however. Furthermore, 'religious nationalism' is not adequate to define Islamic movements such as Khomeinism in Iran, or the Hezbollah or Hamas movements, which focus on Muslim or Shi'i dispossessed (mostaza'f), rather than on the nationals of a particular society. The use of 'Islamic radicalism' is not appropriate either, as there are Islamic radicals, like the Iranian Mujahedin-e Khalgh, who are not fundamentalist and, who, in fact, borrow much modern socialist jargon in constructing their political discourse. 'Islamic populism' might be more appropriate compared with other terms. But it refers only to one aspect of the fundamentalist movements.

'Islamism' might be a convenient term for authors who self-consciously want to avoid offending anybody in the Muslim world. But it is most inadequate, because it lumps together different categories of Islamic activists. Indeed, the term 'Islamists' in a broad sense can encompass three quite different categories of people. Included in the first category are apolitical groups or individuals, including clerics and jurists, or their lay followers, whose activities are limited to seminary schools, mosques, and other religious institutions. This group's main concerns are religious. Apart from innumerable Sunni clerics, the majority of Shi'i clerics in Iran and Iraq historically fall into this category. They are also referred to as 'quietists'. As the Iranian historian Homa Nateq (1984) remarks, many of the top Iranian Shi'i clerics resided in Najaf, Iraq; and they were keener to write in Arabic than in Persian. In the contemporary period, we have the examples of prominent Shi'i clerics such as Grand Ayatollah Abul-Qasim Khu'i and Haj-Agha Rahim Arbab who never involved themselves in politics. In today's 'Islamic' Iran, there are many top clerics who are not political, among them the grand ayatollahs, such as Ayatollah Araki, one of the *Marja' Taqlid* (source of emulation) after Ayatollah Khomeini. During the Iranian Revolution of 1979, Grand Ayatollah Muhammad Kazim Shariatmadari, a moderate close to the Shah (he died under house arrest during Khomeini's rule), formally declared that clerics were beyond politics and they should not involve themselves in the running of the state.

The second category of Islamists are Islamic liberal reformers. These individuals try to reform their societies according to the precepts of Islam, and at the same time to adjust Islam to the needs of modern times. An outstanding example was Muhammad Abduh, the prominent Egyptian theologian and Islamic scholar (Haddad, 1994; Voll, 1991). In contemporary Iran, Ayatollah Taleghani and Mehdi Bazargan's Freedom Movement present good examples of Islamist reformers.

Finally, the third category of Islamists covers the fundamentalists. These are all new movements, with almost no precedent in the Islamic world, with the exception of the Wahhabis of Saudi Arabia. Included in this category are the Muslim Brothers in Egypt and in other Arab countries; Jama'at Islami in India and Pakistan; Velayat-e Faqih and Khomeinism in Iran; the Hezbollah and Hamas movements in Lebanon and the Palestinian Occupied Territories; the National Islamic Front in Sudan; the Islamic Mujahedin and the Taliban in Afghanistan; and the Islamic Salvation Front in Algeria. All these diverse religious-political movements, along with secular national liberation movements, directly or indirectly emerged in reaction to the humiliations experienced by Middle Eastern societies under imperialist domination and later superpower rivalries.

The Muslim Brothers, founded by Hasan al-Bana in 1928 in Egypt, and Jama'at Islami, founded by Abul A'la Mawdudi in 1941 in India before the partition, were both parts of movements which fought against British colonialism. The Iranian Revolution that brought Khomeini and his followers to power in 1979, was a reaction to the United States' dominance in Iran under the Shah. The Harakat al-Mahrumin (Movement of the Dispossessed) and, later, the Afwaj al-Muqawamat al-Lubnaniya (AMAL) in Lebanon were created in response to decades-long deprivation of the Shi'is in Lebanon.[3] Islamic Mujahedin in Afghanistan, before losing power to their yet more brutal rival, the Taliban, came into existence in reaction to the former Soviet Union invasion of Afghanistan. The disillusionment of these movements with post-colonial nationalist governments or autocratic modernizing states in the region inspired the establishment of an 'Islamist' alternative through political action. Participants in these movements felt threatened by the erosion in their countries of traditional beliefs and practices and the growing cultural influence of the West, and attempted to mobilize the Muslim masses around these issues.

Despite ideological, political and cultural differences among Islamic groups and movements in the third category, there exist similarities among them that allow us to refer to them all as fundamentalist. Before depicting characteristic features, however, we need to bear in mind the following points. First, we need to differentiate between the discourse of the founding fathers and the beliefs and practices of their followers. For example, the Egyptian leader Hasan al-Bana not only avoided confrontation with the Egyptian government of his time, but, as David Commins remarks, he tried to fit his vision of Islamic politics within the existing political system (Commins, 1994: 136). By contrast, al-Bana's followers today in Egypt and elsewhere aim at overthrowing the existing state. Radicalization of these movements can be traced to the failure of their reformist agendas and to the brutal reaction of the governments then in power, as exemplified, for example, in the assassination by the Egyptian state of both al-Bana and the prominent ideologue of the Muslim Brothers, Sayyid Qutb.

Second, in approaching fundamentalist movements and regimes, we need to differentiate between the texts and preaching of the leaders and their actual practices – between what they say and what they do. For example, Mawdudi's writings, particularly his emphasis on democracy and the need for state legitimacy in the eyes of society, can easily impress the reader. Mawdudi believed in the Islamization of society prior to the creation of an Islamic state, and believed if 'the state were Islamized before society, then the state would be compelled to resort to autocracy to impose its will on an unwilling and unprepared population' (Nasr, 1997: 106). These views, along with his emphasis on education, rather than force, may sound to activists schooled in the West like Bernstein's 'reformism' in an Islamic context, or it may remind us of Gramsci's emphasis on civil society as a foundation for revolutionary strategy. Mawdudi's language is very misleading, however, considering his extremely reactionary political practice in Pakistan, his views on women and non-Muslim minorities, his opposition to modernizing reforms, and finally his support for the most reactionary and brutal government of Pakistan, that of General Zia ul-Haq. This is why we can never depend on words alone.

At the broadest level, fundamentalism is 'an attitude towards time'. It proposes 'an ideal past, initial conditions' or 'golden age' which contrasts the present and can be retrieved, either by going back to an originating text or 'by the reformation of the society' according to models seen to be copies of an idealized past (Al-Azmeh, 1997: 17). All Islamic fundamentalist movements share the view that the subjugation and subordination of Islamic societies are due to their deviation from 'true' and 'authentic' Islam, occasioned by the quietism and collaboration of the ulama, themselves co-opted by corrupt, infidel and pro-Western regimes. To save and 'purify' Islamic societies, the fundamentalists seek to establish a true Islamic society based on a 'correct' interpretation of the scripture, and modelled after earliest Islamic states under Prophet Muhammad and the four pious khalifs in the seventh century. To attain this goal, the fundamentalists must weaken and overthrow the corrupted state now in power. For this purpose, the most violent and brutal tactics are justified. Once in power, the fundamentalists again, self-righteously, justify the use of absolute and brutal force to suppress their opposition – a feature that Eisenstadt rightly compares with Jacobinism

(Eisenstadt, 1996).[4] Fundamentalist tactics vary. In countries where some sort of democratic structures are in place, like Turkey, they seek through populist and religious slogans to gain seats in the parliament and to form the government. But fundamentalist efforts are much more than political or religious movements. They see Islam as a totalizing force that inspires and regulates all aspects of public and private life. They look to the Qur'an not merely for its moral principles, but to find clues to the future of the world. Fundamentalist movements are similar in that they are determined to subjugate all aspects of human life – be they economic, political, cultural, aesthetic, familial or personal – to the will of God, as declared in religious scripture. Islamist groups insist that they are not only going back to the basics of Islam, but are reviving them as well. They wish to 'revive the hibernating Muslim masses by injecting into their lives, their hearts and minds, the neglected fundamentals of Islam' (Al-Azm, 1993–94 Part I: 97).

A most important characteristic feature of the fundamentalists' perspective is their organic conception of human (religious) societies, a feature which is very briefly referred to by Al-Azmeh. Fundamentalist societies, Al-Azmeh argues, are organic beings which do not change or evolve over time, but only grow and decay. From this viewpoint, elements of such societies are bound together by their own cultures and react to matters culturally imported as a body reacts to the invasion of a parasite. For them, history is cyclical, and the most important feature of political action is one of restoration. It is from this perspective that fundamentalists try to restore their (imagined) golden past, strengthen the local and traditional (read premodern) values and norms, and prevent the penetration and dissemination of any alien or foreign (read modern) values which may contaminate the pure Islamic social body (Al-Azmeh, 1997: 17–21).

Despite some differences,[5] fundamentalist groups share a core of views that I summarize as falling into three interrelated domains: anti-modernity, anti-democracy and anti-feminism. Fundamentalists' anti-modernity originates in their rejection of the Enlightenment. Fundamentalists oppose the separation of religion and politics. They deny the importance of individual rights and are not taken with the notion of universal human progress. In doctrine at least, fundamentalist movements are 'utopian and, past-oriented' (Eisenstadt, 1996). But while they are against the idea of modernity, fundamentalist leaders do not opt for anti-modern living conditions. They send their youth to modern educational institutions in the West and their organizations and parties are modelled after modern political organizations. Still, they insist that the Islamic party is not a political party like other political parties, but is distinguished by being above and beyond political dissent (Al-Azmeh, 1993: 29). Hence, this contradictory reality: seminary students in Qum work with computers and the Internet; there are many different web-sites associated with fundamentalist organizations; the nouveau-riche and powerful mullahs in Iran live in confiscated luxurious mansions and palaces in northern Tehran, and ride around in bullet-proof Mercedes-Benzes. This appetite for modern things has led observers to question the claim that fundamentalists are anti-modern. They fail to see that the fundamentalists are against the ideas and ideals of modernity but not against the products of modernization, which they appreciate and use to establish their premodern social and political order. One wonders, for example, what was more sacred to the Afghan Muja-hedin, their God-given sacred texts or their CIA-delivered, American-given Stinger missile launchers?

Fundamentalists are anti-democratic by virtue of their exclusionary stance. Their attention is focused on the Muslim umma. Following Islamic traditions, they consider non-Muslims as ahl-i thimmi.[6] Non-Muslims may live in the Islamic society, but are, at best, second-class citizens. It is important to note that the thimmi only refers to the followers of major monotheistic religions with claim to a holy, heavenly book and does not include followers of other religions, such as Bahais, or kafars (atheists), who have no rights whatsoever.[7] Even followers of recognized religions, particularly the Jews, have been subject to discrimination, as exemplified by the rampant anti-Semitism of all fundamentalist movements after the creation of the state of Israel. Moreover, since each of these movements considers itself to be the true bearer of 'authentic Islam', even other interpretations of Islam are not tolerated. The Sunni minority in Iran and the Shi'i minority in Saudi Arabia are subject to discrimination, and often persecution. Lack of tolerance is among the outstanding features of the fundamentalists, the most obvious case being Ayatollah Khomeini's *fatwa* against Salman Rushdie.

As for their anti-feminism, fundamentalists share a common sense of threat from changes in gender relations, triggered by the spread of capitalism and feminism. To control women and regain the authority of the patriarchal family are central objectives in the fundamentalist utopia. Fundamentalists of all shapes and creeds, despite their (sometimes much publicized) differences and incompatibilities, set for themselves the same God-given mission of cultural reordering. Society must be changed to revitalize the gendered religious dogma prescribed in holy texts. The ancient moral and ethical boundaries governing man–woman relationships must be re-established. Active participation of individual believers is required in the process. Whatever their differences, Islamic fundamentalists are similar in their views on the place of women in Islamic society. They all feel that because of their natural and biological differences, women should have different roles in the family and society. Even less radical ideologues such as al-Bana emphasize the natural origin of the sexual division of labour. Al-Bana declares that the 'women's place is the home, and her primary roles are mother, wife, and housekeeper'; he prohibits social mixing between the genders (Commins, 1994: 143). For Abul A'la Mawdudi, too, one of the basic human rights is respect for women's chastity; to preserve chastity, women must be kept housebound and in purdah (Mayer, 1995: 100). In fact, once in response to a question whether there had been any particular incident that led Mawdudi to devote himself to Islamic revival, he recounted his horror in returning to Delhi from Hyderabad in 1937 and witnessing a great change among Muslims. That is, they were rapidly moving away from Islam. What indicated this to Mawdudi was unveiled Muslim women: 'I saw Muslim *Surafa* women walking in the streets without *Purdah*, an unthinkable proposition only a few years ago. This change shocked me so greatly that I could not sleep at night, wondering what had brought about this sudden change among the Muslims' (Mawdudi cited in Haq, 1996: 162).

Likewise, Ayatollah Khomeini blamed the Pahlavi dynasty more than anything else for the unveiling of women. He opposed women's recruitment in the public services, claiming that wherever women work they only cause disruption and paralysis of office activities. To mobilize men against women's work outside the home he appealed to traditional male values, asking: 'Do you wish your women to sustain you?' In 1962, Khomeini declared that granting women legal equality on such matters as inheritance and divorce, and removing the restrictions for women to become judges were against the clear instructions of the Qur'an. He called upon the Muslim clergy to express their abhorrence of equal rights for women, and of women's interference (*dekhalat*) in public life, which would inevitably cause social corruption (Khomeini, 1366/1987: 44, 135). Contempt for women's intelligence and emotional and moral stability are revealed in his religious instructions on marriage, divorce and work outside the home and not in his post-revolutionary sermons designed to mobilize the female population in support of the Islamic states.[8]

The most telling signifier of Islamic fundamentalist movements is their commitment to restoring Islamic doctrine and teachings on women's status. To such ends, they dig up medieval Islamic texts prescribing moral codes or invent rules of conduct when the need arises. For example, elements from a dress code practised in past centuries are pronounced 'Islamic' and people are forced to adopt them as a symbol of their 'Islamic identity'. Present-day Iran provides numerous examples of 'Islamic traditions' whose origin, Islamic or otherwise, cannot easily be traced – they must be seen as traditions invented in the service of re-Islamization.

## The Marriage of Premodern and Postmodern Outlooks

Ironically, many arguments used by fundamentalists against the hegemony of the West for pushing forth 'authentic', indigenous traditions are shared by the postmodernist perspective. In this context, Akbar Ahmed is right in arguing that fundamentalism, like postmodernism, is an attempt to resolve how to live in a world of radical doubt. (Ahmed, 1992: 13) That is to say, these two modes of thought, one oriented to the past, the other to the future, end up as political allies in regards to change in Islamic societies. Both postmodernism and Islamic fundamentalism look at social, political and cultural experience in the West and see this historical experience as a damning judgement on the false promises of the Enlightenment. To advance human freedom, both even go so far as to find points in favour of premodern institutions and practices. Both modes of reasoning draw strength by playing with, and, in the case of fundamentalism, manipulating, language and text. But the postmodernist's 'radicalism' very often does not go much beyond a textual, verbal and linguistic shake-up of pre-existing discourse – discourse which appears both as a 'mode of expression' and (as in Said's *Orientalism*) as a set of practices and institutions. This deconstruction of the text identifies the author's conceptual framework and biases involved in its construction, but it does not offer an alternative. As Nederveen Pieterse and Parekh argue, discourse cannot be taken as an all-embracing universe of reality with politics shoved aside as a mere background variable (Nederveen Pieterse and Parekh, 1995: 13–14). The fundamentalists do not confine themselves to the level of discourse. They have a specific agenda which they try to implement. They are determined to use their power, be it legal, political, economic or socio-cultural, in order to achieve their goals. For this purpose they are prepared to use intimidation and physical force.

Islamic fundamentalism also manoeuvres within the sphere of discourse, self-consciously manipulating texts, signs and language in the service of capturing or maintaining popular support. In this regard, the practice of *taqieh* in Shi'ism is especially noteworthy. The Shi'is are a minority within Islam, followers of Imam Ali, the Prophet's son-in-law. Ali was believed to have been unjustly denied the position of khalif after the Prophet's death; he had to isolate himself and await his turn for twenty-three years. In the same way, his followers were forced to conceal their heterodox beliefs and pretend that they were Sunnis. *Taqieh* is a religiously sanctioned form of pretence in which, in the name of a 'higher' or more authentic vision, one says something at the level of 'discourse' while doing (or being) something else in practice. In this context, *Taqieh* can be defined, in postmodern language, as an intentionally falsified discourse which makes 'discourse analysis' a more difficult project. It

would be very difficult, for example, to analyse the discourse of
'Muslim feminists', for we can never determine whether the use of
Islamic signs and vocabulary is a matter of faith or a self-protecting
tactic. Are they truly Muslim women turned feminists or feminists
using Islamic language against 'Islamic' state's repression? Or are
they, instead, Muslim women whose 'feminism' is constructed for
the purpose of softening or sanitizing fundamentalist rule, providing
a striking example of 'Islamic tolerance'?

Other similarities between postmodernists and fundamentalists
include their rejection of the West, their enthusiastic appreciation of
anything non-Western, their localism, their opposition to secularism,
and, as Turner argues, their preference for 'the authenticity of tradition' as compared with 'inherited, imported or alien knowledge'
(Turner, 1994: 7). Hence the disenchantment of both positions with
modern science and scientific achievements, as pillars of modernity,
notwithstanding the willingness to use everything that science and
scientific knowledge have to offer.

Postmodernism and fundamentalism are remarkably close in their
critique of capitalism, although neither reject capitalism altogether
or envisions socialism as a viable alternative. The only difference
between them, perhaps, is that postmodernism offers no alternative
to capitalism, while the fundamentalists serve up a more primitive
capitalism in an Islamic wrap as an alternative to the West's notion
of modernity. Fundamentalism and postmodernism also unite in
their rejection of the excessive consumerism of the West. These points
explain, perhaps, the acceptance of Islam, and sometimes even fundamentalism, by anti-imperialist post-colonial intellectuals in the
West, as the most potent challenge to Western capitalism. They can
also explain the disenchantment of critical intellectuals with secularism more generally, even a return to the deity as an instrument
of human subjectivity in opposition to the objectifying effects of
modernization. Consider, for example, the invocation of God and
the deployment of religious discourse by the postmodernist Luce
Irigaray. To ground their subjectivity, Irigaray suggests, women need
to 'imagine God in their own image', in female form; they need to
project their own image onto the divine (cited in Armour, 1997:
207–10).

This marriage of premodern and postmodern outlooks is a glaring but revealing oddity in our troubled and troubling time. As reflected in discussions about the complex question of women's rights in Islamic societies, and particularly the best strategy in the campaign for improving women's status, the likeness of the two outlooks does not remain at the level of philosophical dialogue alone. They come up with arguments and solutions which may have harmful consequences in the struggle for democracy in the Islamic world and the struggle for women's rights. One such argument is over the analytical and political limits of feminism as the ideology of the women's movement and the universality of women's demands. Ironically, for both postmodernists and fundamentalists, despite their distinct and in many ways opposing views, all ideas and movements find their legitimacy by virtue of their authenticity, both insisting on the relativity of the meanings and standards of oppression. These ideas are very clearly reflected on debates over women and the project of modernity, which will be discussed in the next chapter.

## Notes

1. See, for example, Marty (1995), Mitchell (1987) and Voll (1994).

2. Al-Azm, in his brilliant extensive article, points to 'the epistemological legitimacy, scientific integrity and critical applicability' of terms such as 'fundamentalism' for explaining the new Islamic radical movements. See, Al-Azm (1993–4).

3. I include AMAL as an example of new movements which use religious discourse to radically react to the plight of their people, and not necessarily as fundamentalist. AMAL, under both its celebrated founder, Imam Musa Sadr, and its present leadership, has been a more reformist than fundamentalist movement.

4. Jacobins, the radical deputies during the French Revolution, led by Robespierre, believed that the truth of their vision was sufficient guarantee of their authority to act, and impose their will on the public, using whatever method necessary, including terror and establishment of ruthless minority government.

5. For a useful typology, see Shepard (1987).

6. The followers of other major religions (ahl-i ketab), including Jews, Christians and Zoroastrians, have historically been recognized by Muslim leaders. In the first wave of Islamic expansion, the Copts and the Jews were given protection, subject to the recognition of Islamic rule and payment of

head taxes. Under subsequent Islamic empires, particularly under the Ottomans, the thimmi had the right to practise their religion under their own religious patriarchs.

7. For a very illuminating discussion of the rights of non-Muslims in contemporary Islamic societies, see Mayer (1995).

8. For Khomeini's views on women's legal rights in the family, see problems no. 450–60 and 2424–544 (Khomeini, 1980).

# Chapter 5

# Women, Modernity and Social Change

Feminists have long argued that the outcome of modernity, associated with the set of ideas and worldviews known as the Enlightenment, has been paradoxical for women. The recognition of individual freedom, whether defined as freedom from 'dogma and intolerence' and from religious institutions which allowed the new 'rational and scientific man' to investigate the mysteries of nature (Hall, 1996: 603), or 'freedom from scarcity, want, and the arbitrariness of nature', was a human achievement providing the possibility for individuals to work 'freely and creatively for the pursuit of human emancipation and the enrichment of daily life' (Harvey, 1990: 12). Defence of individual freedom, however, required the recognition of individual 'rights' vis-à-vis the state, including the right to privacy and to private property, which the state is bound to secure. The distinction between the state (public) and the individual (private) required the recognition of 'the Power of a Father over his Children, a Master over his Servant, a Husband over his Wife, and a Lord over his Slave' (Locke cited in Marshal, 1994: 11). 'The privatization of the family, and the legitimation of patriarchal authority in the private sphere', feminists argue, which positioned the individual 'as prior to and partially outside of society, permitted the exclusion of women from society'. For 'it was only the male who became individuated outside the family, and thus it was males, and male activity, that constituted the public sphere of "society"' (Marshal, 1994: 11, 14). Thus modernity was emancipatory to men but oppressive to women. It was empowering

to men but overpowering to women. Arguing that the French Revolution, and even the revolutionary ideas of equality, were masculinist
projects, feminists highlight the discriminatory, male-centred and
Eurocentric character of the movement.

The Revolution, it is argued, was proclaimed for a narrow con-
stituency. While attacking old bases of economic pivilege and political
power, the Enlightenment's singular concern with legal rights and
privacy of conscience still left room for all kinds of inequalities.
Bourgeois reforms reinforced sex and race subjugation. Recognizing
equality of rights for men born equal had the effect of making
bourgeois, white, European, heterosexual man 'the universal human
subject'. It was his worldviews and values which then became the
reference point for the rest of humanity. By racializing humanity
and by excluding women, notions of political rights and equality
turned inward and became contradictory. Full citizenship was denied
to women, enslaved Africans and other colonized people. Women
were declared to be non-citizens. Their political clubs were shut
down (Kandall, 1988; Tijssen, 1991). Modernity created the modern
man, leaving women behind. Hence, modernism and modernity were
illusory projects. The perfection of humanity was promised, but
conveniently postponed to a later date.

The impact on women of capitalism and modern industry is also
believed to have been ambiguous. Capitalism advanced by commer-
cializing human productive activities. It rationalized the market,
separating the domestic and private from the public and social. At
the same time, the relentless drive for 'efficiency' undermined traditional notions of a male-centred household wage, forcing women
(and children) of poor classes – and later large section of middle-
class women – into paid work.[1] In some ways, capitalism opened
new opportunities to women – including the possibility of survival
outside the family, challenging the patriarchal domination of the
individual man. But bourgeois rule did not challenge patriarchy or
male power. The pre-capitalist sexual division of labour took a new
form. It was not abolished, but, rather, modernized, and used to
keep women's productive and reproductive capacities under control.
Patriarchy predated capitalism. But the advance of modern industry
would not, by itself, create a sex- and race-blind army of proletariat,

as Marx and Engels had argued. Indeed, as Janet Sayers notes, many feminists argue that Engels was 'unduly optimistic' in his analysis that the family would alter and full equality between the sexes would result from the technological advance, and the transition to socialism (Sayers, 1986: 57–8). Industrial capitalism, in fact, shattered the productive unit of husband and wife. Initially, at least, women became more dependent on men for economic survival. Marriage for women, as Hamilton notes, became women's 'food ticket, and an inadequate and shaky one at that' (Hamilton, 1980: 40). Capitalism and patriarchy are two interlocking systems; hence, there is a relationship between wage labour and domestic labour: 'the hierarchical domestic division of labour is perpetuated by the labour market and vice versa' (Hartman, 1979: 208).

Moreover, as Ehrenreich and English have argued, the establishment of modern industry and 'the triumph of the Market' undermined women's traditional productive roles within the family which were essential to its survival and society's well-being.

> The old unity of work and home, production and family life, was necessarily and decisively ruptured. Henceforth the household would no longer be a more or less self-contained unit, binding its members together in common work. When the production entered the factory, the household was left with only the modest personal biological activities – eating, sex, sleeping, the care of small children, the sick and the aged. (Ehrenreich and English, 1979: 10)

Hence, the division between two distinct spheres, public and private, and the initial dependence of women on men for economic survival. As the economy became commercialized, 'female traditional skills, such as baking, brewing, and preparing herbal medicine, were lost; and the new industrial society was reshaped in a way that ensured the dominance of male ideas and interests in the public world of work and politics' (Bradley, 1996: 128). Distinguishing two main forms of patriarchy, private and public, Sylvia Walby argues that in the household women's labour is expropriated by individual patriarchs, 'while in the public form it is a more collective appropriation'. With the changes associated with industrial capitalism, the household is no longer the chief site of patriarchal relations, although both structures are still present (Walby, 1990: 24).

However, I want to argue that while the brutally exploitative and discriminatory nature of bourgeois development shakes our confidence in the advances and triumphs of 'modernism' and modernity, it can hardly convince us of the superiority of the 'good old days' and the advantages of premodern social formations for women. None of the arguments put forth proves that women enjoyed an autonomous, humane and fulfilling life in premodern societies. Capitalism and modern industry have invoked a two-sided process. While entry into the workforce exposed women to exploitation, it broke down male power and control within the family and challenged overtly misogynist social and legal practices which denied to women full citizenship status. Hence, Marx's declaration still holds true that

> As horrendous and disgusting as the disintegration of the old family system within capitalism appears to be, modern industry, by involving women and young people of both sexes in the socially organized production processes outside of domestic sphere, has, nevertheless, created the economic basis for a higher form of the family and the relationship between the two sexes. (Marx, 1983: 372–3)

In bringing in these developments, capitalism, for Marx, was acting as the 'unconscious tool' of history, destroying the old relations and creating new ones. Marx's assertion that 'everything seems pregnant with its contradictions' is as true now as it was then. The public domain has become the primary site for women to demand removal of legal and social obstacles to gender equity, providing the terrain for more effective collective struggle.

There is little doubt that capitalism, in itself, cannot secure gender equality. Improvements in women's legal and social status in the West have been partial, conditional and formal, what Alexandra Kollontai has called 'an equal share of inequalities' or equality vis-à-vis men of the same class (Kollontai, 1977: 58–9). It is also true that women, particularly in advanced capitalist societies, have been released from male domestic bondage with the promise of freedom, but this freedom has brought new, sometimes terrifying, consequences. The pressure to live up to the images depicted by the media, the beauty trap, increased gender violence, and the reduced human reciprocity which accompanies bourgeois individualism – all raise doubts about 'modern life' and the 'modern woman'.

Still, it is disturbingly misleading to argue, as does Akbar Ahmed, for example, that gender violence is the inevitable outcome of modernity, or that rape, mutilation and abuse are 'the destiny of the postmodern female' – that 'there is an inherent tendency in Western society to view women as hate objects' (A. Ahmed, 1992: 247–8). Ahmed recites these ills of modern life in order to ask why Muslims should be 'dragged along the path of social experimentation which they know to be diverging from their own vision of society? Why should they disrupt their domestic situation for temporary values, however overpowering?' (A. Ahmed, 1992: 257)

Ahmed's account is one-sided. He does not understand that the conflicts, contradictions and upheavals in gender relations are the inevitable outcome of a modernization process which involves profound changes in male and female roles. He does not see that the increase in gender violence expresses the profound insecurity which men feel as a result of the legal and social advance in women's rights, and the challenge to male power by gender-conscious women who have truly shaken up Western societies. Instead, changes in Western family relations, gender conflict and domestic clashes are attributed to a media conspiracy:

> If the power of the Western media dictated the 1980s social agenda – feminism, homosexuality, Aids – we are, in the 1990s, already discussing post-feminism, post-homosexuality and post-Aids. Many of the issues which Islam has never conceded, such as the use of alcohol and drugs, are now being widely re-accepted in the West. (Ahmed, 1992: 257)

Ahmed is concerned for the stability of the family as 'the core of the Muslim social structure', which is weakened in his view by such 'Western' factors as divorce, the challenge to parents, the marginalization of older people, and the regular shifting of the home. This argument seems to assume that gender violence and rape, the sexual molestation of children and the gruesome murder of women do not occur in the Islamic world. But the reality is that the absence of a free press and independent media in most Islamic societies, a male-serving value system which decides what issues get reported, and the vigilantly guarded cultural taboos which forbid the exposure of family secrets make it hard in the Middle East for gender violence to come to public attention. Hence, the more terrifying forms of violence against women are perceived as being unique to the West. Nonetheless, even the sparse reports that we get on violent crimes committed against women in Islamic societies make self-congratulatory accounts of the 'terrible state of women's lives in Europe and North America' unwarranted.[2] As well, we would see more clearly the sorry state of women's lives in Islamic societies[3] if we stopped identifying as 'cultural practices' various forms of traditional or state-enforced gender violence, including honour killing, stoning of women to death on charges of adultery and fornication, public lashing for improper veiling, child marriage and female genital mutilation. These are *legally sanctioned* gender crimes, even though they are not so considered by Muslim rulers and community leaders.

Ahmed, to his credit, does not suggest that the most viable option for Muslims is a 'retreat accompanied by passionate expressions of faith and anger'. He is even critical of self-styled Muslim intellectuals who, in their rejection of Orientalism, have created Occidentalism, or 'Orientalism in reverse', as Sadiq Al-Azm (1981) would put it. The problem, however, is the style of thought that Ahmed represents – that is, a selective and highly critical presentation of what modernity has entailed for women in the West, combined with a nostalgic and exceptionally romantic notion of experiences of women in the Islamic world. Which is to say, if modernity and practices associated with modern values appear to have had no positive aspects and have only furthered women's sexual abuse, economic exploitation and cultural alienation, it is because romantic, anti-Orientalist authors present it in that way. For example, why not talk of how modernizing efforts have challenged patriarchal authority and gender power?

It can be argued, as postmodernists do, that modern forms of domination and non-freedoms have replaced premodern forms. Under the present circumstances, the majority of women in the Middle East and North Africa have not fully benefited from the forces of modernism, despite the fact that their lives have been touched by modernization processes, one way or another. But this is because modernization projects in the Middle East over the last hundred years have excluded genuinely transformative changes in gender relations. As Sharabi notes, 'the patriarchal structures of Arab Society, far from having been truly modernized, have only been reshaped and preserved in "modernized" forms.' He goes on to argue that European conquest and colonization of the Arab world have served to speed up material modernization. But 'it has at the same time greatly contributed to reinforcing patriarchal authority and institutions as well as the inner relations of patriarchalism' (Sharabi, 1992: 129). Sharabi suggests that in the Arab world, as in many other Third World societies, 'the marriage of imperialism and patriarchy produced not genuine modernity but helped instead to create a hybrid sort of society/culture, a kind of "modernized" patriarchy, namely *neopatriarchy*.' Along the same lines, Fatima Mernissi identifies the process as a 'mutilated modernity, void of the great democratic advances' (Mernissi, 1992: 113).

The same can be said about Iran, where the modernization process did not create the socio-economic structures necessary for a change in gender relations. As I argue elsewhere, the persistence of pre-capitalist, pre-industrial socio-cultural and political structures, including Islamic practices and legal traditions guarded by the Shi'i clergy, were not conducive to changing gender roles and to transforming relations of domination and subordination between the sexes. Quite the contrary. The modernizing state, as 'the big patriarch', co-opted women's quest for equity, generated and reinforced class division among women, and fragmented women's rights activists. The all-embracing patriarchal culture with its far-reaching and entrenched sexist norms directly influenced women's activities in public spaces, in political parties, and in cultural life. The post-revolutionary events and Islamization policies of the Iranian state illuminate the incomplete, deformed and debased character of the 'modernity' which the *ancien régime* championed (Moghissi, 1994).

None of these realities, however, leads us to the conclusion that modernism was destructive or even dismal for women. The anti-modernists still have to tell us what Middle Eastern women will gain by rejecting the ideas, values and institutions associated with modernity. They could begin, perhaps, by clearly defining the categories of rights that women have achieved in the West which are irrelevant to the experiences of women in Islamic societies. Or they could at least identify the liberatory aspects of the 'culturally differ-ent' Islamic gender beliefs and practices which should be celebrated and preserved.

## Mystification of 'Islamic Traditions'

To counter theorizing on the Middle East which focuses exclusively on the subjugation of women by Muslim men, it is important to reveal those aspects of women's lives which have been neglected or eliminated entirely from research. Most importantly, the contradiction between domination of women and women's resistance to it has to be acknowledged and valued. As Lazreg puts it, we need to see women's lives, even under adversity, as 'meaningful, coherent and understandable, instead of being infused "by us" with doom and sorrow.' It is also important to draw attention to the fact that 'the other is just as entitled as I am to her/his humanity expressed in his/her cultural mode' (Lazreg, 1990: 339). But there is an important distinction to be made between a sympathetic affirmation of an-other person's culture and a romantic indulgence which feeds on nostalgia or creates a myth. In emphasizing the humanity of the local and the life-affirming character of 'indigenous' cultural modes, it is incautious to lose oneself in fantasy or to over-emphasize cultural modes which are exotic or different. For this might unknowingly block initiatives for change.

In fact, the glorified conception of whatever is non-Western propels intellectuals who oppose Orientalism to rise to the defence of the most backward, oppressive institutions in non-Western societies, the Middle East included. Rather than objecting to the representation of the Islamic world in the Western media, which sometimes makes the whole region appear as a large veiled harem, some Middle Eastern scholars rise, instead, to the defence of the very institutions of veil, harem and polygamy. The position of an anthropologist, Homa Hoodfar, is instructive enough to merit a more detailed examination.

Hoodfar takes issue with the dominant views and misconceptions about Muslim women and the veil in the West. She criticizes the Orientalists' image-making and 'imagination'; finds faults with whatever the 'Westerners' have said about women's situation in the Islamic societies; blames the colonialists for all the problems faced by women; and tries to counter these wrongs by constructing new images for 'Muslim women', Islamic institutions and Islamic societies – images whose correspondence to reality is debatable. In a review of the history of the veil in Islamic societies, for instance, Hoodfar first tells us that the veil is not a Qur'anic phenomenon, and that 'it was not until the reign of Safavids (1501–1722) in Iran and the Ottoman Empire (1357–1924) that 'the veil emerged as a widespread symbol of status among the Muslim ruling class'. The veil became more widespread in the nineteenth century. 'Muslims have justified it in the name of Islam', but only after it was 'promoted by the colonials as a symbol of Muslim societies' (Hoodfar, 1993: 6).

As I discussed in Chapter 1, the role of the colonial powers in solidifying Islamic gender practices has been established by feminist historical researchers. But by offering a very broad definition of the veil – one that, for example, includes also the 'traditional male clothing of much of the Arab world' – Hoodfar mystifies the clear meaning of the veil, that is, a garment which controls and confines women's space. For Hoodfar, the culprits in women's veiling and seclusion and the imposition of unequal status are to be found outside Islamic institutions and practices – the 'modern states', the 'paternalist rulers,' the 'authorities' who made 'the clothing more gender-specific', and in 'the westernization and colonization of Muslim societies' which created the 'most drastic difference between male and female clothing worn among the Arab urban elite'. Hoodfar blames the Western literature on the subject, which has not under-stood the 'multiple reasons' for the veil. Completely innocent are Islamic beliefs and practices and the clerics who have painstakingly protected them for many centuries against modern ideas, institu-tions and relations. Even when Hoodfar refers to 'the religious au-thorities' who opposed changes in favour of women 'in the name of religion', she does not find the heart to count them as active agents in sustaining women's degraded position. They are forgiven because they were simply reacting to the 'strategic mistakes' of 're-formists and modernizers', who combined 'unveiling and formal education in one package' (Hoodfar, 1993: 8–9).

Hoodfar castigates the Western 'imagination' also for 'excluding the reality of harems and for the way women experienced them' and for representing the harem as 'a place where Muslim men imprisoned their wives', where women 'had nothing to do except beautify themselves and cater to their husbands' huge sexual appetite'. She objects to such representations because they 'exclude the reality of harems and the way women experienced them' (Hoodfar, 1993: 8) – an experience which another author, Leila Ahmed, also reconstructs as the women's 'protected space', a place where the sense of collectivity and bonding among women was increased (Ahmed, 1982: 521–34).

This is not to say that the common Western view of the harem was not distorted. As Keddie notes, the harem was far from the den of idleness and the sexual paradise fantasized about by the Western viewer; the term 'harem' 'does not have sexy connotations, but means the part of the house forbidden to men who are not close relatives'. For the middle-class men who were not polygamous, Keddie writes 'the *harem* was where the indoor work of the family was planned and carried on, usually under the supervision of the wife of the eldest male' (Keddie and Baron, 1991: 11). Nonetheless, in the polygamous and prosperous elite household women's experience in the harem was not any better than life in a prison. A nineteenth-century document involving the written instructions of an Iranian lord to his steward before leaving on a journey provides a revealing account of life in a harem. No amount of intellectual acrobatics can turn this into an empowering experience for women. The document reads:

> The entrance to my interior [*andaroun* – women's quarter] should always be closed, the chastity and maidenliness of my housemaids [wives] must be observed more strictly than when I am present. No voice of chatting and singing should be heard from the interior. My wives should not be seen at the roof-top or the terrace; they should not go for a walk and should not promenade in the garden. If they do otherwise, the elder gatekeeper should bring a stick, put them in a gunny sack, and beat the hell out of them. (Nateq, 1350/1980: 15)

Not surprisingly, from this conceptual framework originates Hoodfar's assessment of the modernizing experiments in Iran under Reza Shah and his son, the last Shah. Hoodfar's condemnation of the unveiling of women under Reza Shah is well justified. The government-led unveiling created enormous problems for traditional women. The policy was carried out through coercion – the only method in nation-building which the region's modernizers like Reza Shah mastered. It was not implemented through consensus-building or by making use of the educational and resocialization apparatuses or with the engaged support of the pioneers of the Iranian women's movement. However, what is notable here is that unveiling was not entirely the result of Reza Shah's or the colonialists' desire. It was a response, however authoritarian and self-serving, to a long-sought-after goal of Iranian intellectuals of both genders.

In fact, unveiling was the subject of much debate during the nineteenth century. Since the late 1920s Iranian women activists, teachers and artists, like their sisters in Egypt, stopped wearing the veil in public before it became state policy. Reza Shah's anti-veil offensive did not come about until 1936, only after much resistance to the anti-veil campaigns of women themselves, including the petition produced by the Patriotic Women's League in the early 1930s (Nateq, 1358/1980: 45–53; Sanasarian, 1983: 14–16). On all this Hoodfar is silent. This raises the question as to in whose interests is it, except the present-day champions of the reveiling of Iranian women, to present unveiling in Iran as a concocted colonialist ploy, executed by the local, Westoxicated modernizer, Reza Shah?

By drawing upon the experiences of a few members of her own family in a small town in west-central Iran, Hoodfar draws the conclusion that unveiling caused cultural alienation and unnecessary practical hardships for women. The negative aspects of unveiling, particularly for women from religious urban middle-class families, is not in doubt. But Hoodfar's argument is problematic on several accounts. First, she takes for granted that all women in Iran were veiled prior to Reza Shah's unveiling order. This is simply not true. The veil was an urban phenomenon. Women of ethnic minorities, such as the Kurds, and women from the villages and from northern Iran were not veiled. In fact, the published records of the unveiling policy by the Iran National Archives show that this fact was also known to the authorities at the time, and it was reflected in their instructions to the authorities in certain provincial cities (Iran

National Archives, 1371/1993). Which is to say, the experiences of female members of Hoodfar's family cannot be extended to all women in Iran. For example, my mother, who was born in a small city in the Caspian area and was raised in a rather well-to-do family with government connections, does not recall any period in her life when she was forced to wear the veil. Therefore, the unveiling exercise did not constitute a dramatic change in her appearance or lifestyle. Second, Hoodfar depicts a very romanticized picture of religious women before unveiling, obscuring the positive and liberating impact of unveiling for millions of Iranian women who in subsequent decades gradually came to benefit from enlarged educational and employment opportunities. Unveiling also had a liberating effect for women of religious minorities, particularly the Jews, who, as a result of the anti-Semitic practices of the Shi'i clerics, were not allowed to appear veiled in public, in order to distinguish the Other woman from Muslim ones. Before Reza Shah's modernization policies weakening the clerical power, Jews were considered 'unclean' (*najjes*), were not allowed to touch foodstuffs, and, among other restrictions, were not allowed, for example, to leave home and mingle with Muslims on rainy days.[4] Unveiling helped eliminate overt discrimination on religious grounds. With the secularization of the administrative and judicial systems, other steps were also taken in favour of religious minorities. These came to a halt with the rise of Islamic fundamentalism to power.

In a similar way, Neyereh Tohidi takes note of the 'deformed nature' and 'the distorted character' of capitalist developement and modernization in Iran between the 1950s and 1970s. Because of the 'unevenness' of these changes, feminist consciousness did not advance. Tohidi argues that 'the conception, objectives, and strategy of feminism in different nations and regions have become intertwined with very different economic, socio-cultural, and political conditions' (Tohidi, 1994: 110), concluding on this basis that women's consciousness and women's demands in developing countries are different in kind from those emerging in advanced capitalist societies. Tohidi argues that even the 'strategic objectives' of feminism (using Karen Sacks' categorization – economic autonomy; access to power and authority; a single uniform sexual standard; the ending of invidious stereotypes of gender) are 'conceptualized' differently in different regions, or do not apply at all to the Third World. This claim is problematic and runs into serious difficulties when applied, for example, to the case of Iran. For Tohidi argues that 'a completely successful bourgeois-democratic revolution, during the 1906–11 Constitutional Movement, entailing industrialization, economic advancement, political development could have democratized and secularized the then semi-feudal society of Iran', and could have led, eventually, to 'economic autonomy, political and social sophistication of women, individuation, and eradiction of suffocating patrimonial familial traditions, all paving the way for women's emancipation' (Tohidi, 1994: 115). Tohidi is not, perhaps, aware that with this argument she has pulled the rug out from under her claim that feminisms must be different in advanced capitalist and Third World societies. Using Tohidi's own example we get caught in a contradictory argument which discards her theory of 'First World' and 'Third World' feminisms. Because if with a 'total' and 'full' development of capitalism Iranian women could have achieved their political and economic demands, then there would not have been a difference between them and the women in advanced capitalist societies. Tohidi's argument is also problematic because it seems that, for her, capitalist development must be 'fully' and 'totally' dominant before it can have effects on social and economic structures and relations. That capitalism and industrialization was not an 'all-encompassing' process in Iran is a fact. But it is also a fact that, nonetheless, despite its not being 'total' and 'fully' dominant, capitalism changed many social structures and relations in the country, changes which favoured improvements in women's status. My concern, however, is somewhere else.

In using 'nations' and 'cultures' as the unit of analysis, class differences among women which defines needs, aspirations and demands are completely ignored. What Tohidi sees as the demands of 'women' in advanced industrial societies apply more exactly to the needs of specific groups (mostly urban middle-class women). In advanced industrial societies, many poor, non-white and working-class women – like the majority of women in Third World countries – have immediate demands that are rather different and are related to their own and their families' basic survival needs. On the other hand, many educated middle-class women of Third World and Middle Eastern societies share the same career aspirations and personal demands that Karen Sacks categorizes as strategic objectives, and to which Tohidi refers as First World feminist goals. The history of women's movements in such countries as Egypt and Iran, which I will briefly discuss in Chapter 7, points to the fact that educated women in these societies articulated similar demands from the 1930s onward.

The point is that it is one thing to challenge the negative colonial imagery of women in Islamic societies as helpless, frail, uneducated, passive. It is quite another thing to reverse the argument and construct one that celebrates Islamic traditions and obscures their gender-biases and oppressive consequences for women. As an example of such a view we can look at Anouar Majid's discussion of feminism in Islam. Majid's hostility towards feminism and the idea of women's individual rights and autonomy prompts him to mystify the reactionary character of Islamic patriarchal institutions, past and present. In his romantic account of the Islamic stand on women's rights he constructs a delusory pro-woman's liberation history for the *ulama* (for example in 'pre-Westernized' Egypt) to fit his even more delusive narrative of the *ulama*'s rule in contemporary Islamic societies like Iran. The harem, he claims, did not prevent women in Egypt from conducting business deals. In fact, '[a]llied with *ulama* women exercised *sufficient* [my emphasis] control over their lives' (Majid, 1998). But as the history of the women's movement in Islamic societies, including Egypt, demonstrates, women did not consider their rights and status and the public space open to them as *sufficient* as Majid does. They demanded equal citizenship status – something which Majid seems not to find necessary or being in cultural harmony with Islamic societies.

The Islamic solution is for Majid the only solution. He suggests that secular Middle Eastern intellectuals are infected by 'orientalist prejudices' (Majid, 1998: 353); the critical analyses of Islamic concepts of human rights and democracy by feminist scholars like Fatima Mernissi and Elizabeth Mayer are of 'limited value' because they embrace a 'bourgeois notion of democracy and individual liberties', accepting the 'bourgeois definition of human rights in the West' (Majid, 1998: 328, 346); Iranian women who resist imposition of Islamic dress codes are simply 'upper-class women conforming to trends in international fashion' (Majid, 1998: 338). Majid celebrates women's agency and empowerment within a protected and narrowly defined women's space, but neglects more crucial spaces, larger socio-cultural structures, and religious and politico-legal institutions in which women are robbed of both agency and any prospect for meaningful change. He justifies the systemic brutalization of women in his ideal Islamic state, Iran, and naturally he has to lash out against all those who do not share his faith in 'the Islamic solution.'

Majid proposes a 'third way', which 'synthesizes' 'modernist ideologies' and 'clerical Islam', making Islam, by this stroke, 'democratic, anti-patriarchal and anti-imperialist', based on 'the equal status and dynamic contributions of women and extending full rights to minorities' (Majid, 1998: 324–5). How, then, to reconcile this vision with Majid's support for fundamentalist regimes like the Islamic Republic of Iran, which he claims is the centre of 'thriving intellectual debates over how to challenge repressive laws from within the Islamic tradition itself'? (Majid, 1998: 355).

In nearly all Islamic countries, women constitute the front-line fighters in the battle of Middle Eastern intellectuals against aggressive state terrorism and Islamic fanaticism. From Indonesia to the Arab Emirates, from Iran to Algeria, women are the target of the violence of religious fanatics and of Islamic states because they oppose an oppressive religious tradition and a 'culturally specific' justice system which denies their basic rights. These women aspire to and are entitled to the same rights that women enjoy in the West, including basic equality in the law of marriage and divorce and in the disposition of child custody, as well as protection against legally sanctioned forms of violence within the family. Regardless of how unhappy one may be with the extent and pace of development in women's status in the West, European and North American societies have provided women, at least, with an elementary formal standing as legal agents and with a minimum protection against physical brutality. To the vast majority of women in many cultures outside Europe or North America these rights are denied. The insistence, out of context, on the cultural specificity of women's concerns and the privileging of the voices of religion make such rights even more difficult to achieve.

## Feminism Revisited

Feminism, like other ideological and social movements, has a contingent nature. It takes different forms when articulated with different social, economic and cultural systems and levels of development. Does this lead us to a rejection of the universal claims for feminism or feminist 'objectives' and 'strategies'? This is not to say that gender is the common *essence* which binds all women together. Feminists have long accepted the fact that women's experience of gender is always influenced by their particular class, race, sexual and national location. As Linda Nicholson and Steven Seidman, among others, argue, identities are multiple, unstable and interlocking, and there is 'no separate, independent "women's" experience that could be marked off and presumed as the ground of feminist politics.' Pointing out the limits of a feminist epistemology that is grounded in a concept of essential female identity, Nicholson and Seidman argue that such epistemology is normative and exclusionary because it cannot give expression to all women's experience (Nicholson and Seidman, 1995: 27–8).

I sympathize with attempts to take into account other forms of oppression from which women suffer and to count the diversity, difference and even conflicts among women. But I think women *as* women have definable interests and concerns that can form the basis for solidarity, common action and common struggle among women. This is why we can consider feminism as a universal movement against sexism (which takes different forms and is practised with differing rigour in different societies). But because we do not assume a pregiven unity among women *as* women, those women who for various reasons stand on the side of the oppressors are excluded from this solidarity and common struggle. However, if we are wrong to talk of women as being oppressed and discriminated against *as* women, as a result of sexism in patriarchal societies – that is, in all known human societies – then we should, perhaps, abondon gender-based politics altogether. That is to say, women, as members of a particular race, class, sexual and national group, will make alliances with other members of their own groups against the particular oppression they are subjected to. Why should we use a feminist frame of reference at all? That is, what is at stake here is the gender-based struggle. If gender is so insignificant in women's experience as members of particular racial, class and national groups, then we should do away with gender-based politics and feminism altogether.

I want to argue that if we go down this road we will end up excluding women of developing societies from the movement's emancipatory ideals and goals. True, women in these societies suffer from multiple forms of oppression, some demonstrably more brutal than gender oppression. Women's struggle, then, has to set for itself different priorities and take up different strategies and make different alliances. But can we then say that gender-based politics and ideals are the privileged domain of better-off women in advanced industrial societies? For example, by not recognizing the legitimacy and the vitality of women's voices within the Islamic world who seek the same developments in their countries as feminists do in industrially advanced societies, would we not adopt a double standard in dealing with non-Western peoples and cultures? Would not such an argument lead to a new form of ethnocentrism under the guise of countering Eurocentric and ethnocentric outlooks?

Two points are important to note here. First, many of the obstacles which prevail today in the Islamic world existed in the earlier stages of capitalist development in Europe. Women's exclusion from education, restrictions in employment, denial of female suffrage, legally sanctioned marital rape and violence, lack of child custody and rigid gendered moral codes are obvious examples. To remove these obstacles, after much struggle by feminists and social reformers, has been a defining test for modernity. Many of the bourgeois reforms in the areas of education, health, working conditions, family legislation, and so forth, were not conceivable in pre-capitalist societies. Not long ago debates over sexuality and the need for women's control over their bodies were off-limits topics for activists, academics and the public. It has been a major achievement for feminists in the West (and increasingly, though cautiously and timidly, in non-

Western societies as well) to place these subjects at the centre of public debates. To be sure, women's lack of control over their bodies and the sexual exploitation and abuse of women is an area of which women, North and South, have much common experience, and which could be a major ground for a world-wide feminist coalitional politics.

Now, we should ask whether demanding to have control over one's own body and the right to sexual expression, as advocated by feminists in the West, is something irrelevant to the lives of women in the Islamic world. Some gender activists from Muslim societies may suggest so. For example, Fatima Ebrahim, a secular Sudanese socialist and a long time woman's rights advocate and President of Women's Union (WU), asks: 'what priority can sexual choice have to a woman whose child is dying of hunger?' Ebrahim also makes it clear that she deliberately projected herself as 'a traditional, respect-ful, family oriented Muslim woman' in order to gain credibility in public (cited in Hale, 1996: 172–4).[5] But only individuals who have somehow escaped the sexual repression which dominates the lives of women and men in Islamic societies can deny its overriding role in defining women's experience. Poverty and hunger hang over women's heads throughout the region. But female persecution for their 'bad' *hejab* and barbaric practices such as honour killing and stoning women to death show that sexuality and sexual repression are where women suffer most.

Second, I find the arguments which present feminism as Western, middle-class, uni-focused and, hence, apolitical increasingly in-accurate, to say the least. This is not to deny the historical blindness of feminism to issues of race, class or the unfortunate growth of the separatist, self-indulgent and identity-concerned trends within femi-nism. It is only to challenge the charge that only non-white, non-European feminism is political or takes up the issues of racial, class and national oppression seriously. Several hunger marches organized by feminists in Canada in the last few years, and many coalitions formed against the Conservative government's war on the poor in various provinces in opposition to unleashed privatization, demon-strate that feminists are now taking on many issues as feminist concerns to which they were oblivious previously. This has restored my confidence in feminism – and I know I am not alone – as a most potent social movement of our time for justice, democracy and equity.

The variability and complexities of women's concerns in different countries, nationalities, cultures and religions should not cloud the reality that 'no other feature of the pre-modern scene has persisted so stubbornly as male dominance', and that 'the repudiation of unearned privilege with its implication for gender relations is an integral part of the package of modernity' (Lovibond, 1989: 12). Feminist ideals, goals and strategies can be and should be formulated in many different forms, according to differing social, cultural and political contexts. Today we no longer find it constructive to insist on the modernist idea of 'sameness' in men and women as a basis for claiming equal rights. Feminists now stress differences between men and women and among women. They define equality as 'indifference to difference for the purposes of ending legal and economic discrimination' (Ebert, 1996: 154). But if, in the West, these differences between men and women do not count much or count less than in the past, at least in certain important areas of social life this has been the direct outcome of women's legal victories. The legal, social and cultural rights which women enjoy in the West, as compared with their sisters elsewhere, are a consequence of the recognition of women's full citizenship status (personhood) – that is, equality before the law, and equality in law. True, these developments did not always keep pace with the project of modernity. But their materialization, in the course of time, was closely associated with the recognition in the West of individual rights, separation of church from state, and the rule of law rather than the rule of the divine – all of which originated from the political ideas and political institutions central to the Enlightenment, universalism and the project of modernity.

## Notes

1. Researchers on black women in America have challenged the notion of a private/public dichotomy as well as the universality of the nuclear family form. Such splits between domestic and public labour did not exist

for black women in America, who have always worked in the fields, in mines, in the factory and as domestic labourers. Among many sources, see Davis (1981: 3–29) and Hill Collins (1991: 46–58).

2. See, for example, the crimes reported in Chapter 2 n. 4. It should go without saying that there are numerous cases which do not appear in the newspapers. The number of women imprisoned in Pakistan since the introduction of the Islamic penal system has alarmingly increased. Women prisoners are routinely subject to physical and sexual abuse by Muslim policemen (Haq, 1996: 174–5). Horrifying crimes against Algerian women, such as axing them to death, cutting off their breasts and taking young women as 'sex slaves' and killing them later, are also the routine practice of terrorists struggling for the establishment of a 'truly Islamic society' (*Guardian Weekly*, 1998).

3. The murder of women to protect 'family honour' is prevalent throughout the Middle East. A report by the Al-Fanar Palestinian feminist organization estimates the number of murders or attempted murders to be within the range of twenty to forty cases a year in Palestinian society (Al-Fanar Report, 1995). See also Abu-Odeh (1996). An unprecedented increase in the number of violent crimes committed against women under the pretext of defending 'family honor' has alarmed even Iranian officials. In 1997 (1376), in Ahvaz alone, fifty-two cases of honour killings were reported (*Shahrvand*, 22 May 1998).

4. For an excellent collection of articles on Iranian Jews, see Sarshar (1996).

5. In fact, the WU constitution stresses that members must be morally virtuous and that 'it excludes anyone who has an Afro hairstyle and jeans'. I am grateful to Amani el Jack for bringing this point to my attention.

# Chapter 6

# Fundamentalists in Power: Conflict and Compromise

Iran under Islamic fundamentalism represents, perhaps, one of the wonders of the world. Women and men are in segregated public spaces. There is forced veiling, and employment and educational policies are discriminatory. Families are ruled by archaic legislation. The criminal law includes stoning of women to death, a punishment taken from orthodox Islamic texts and the *Shari'a*. On the other hand, there are reports of an increase in the visibility and professional activities of 'Muslim women'. 'Women in black *chador*' now represent Islamic Iran at international conferences and on state visits, addressing issues of interest to feminism globally, such as economic development, birth control, gender violence and women's human rights; we even saw a veiled 'Muslim woman' carrying the Iranian banner in the 1996 Olympics. 'Muslim women' in Iran, we are told, can today go as high up the professional and bureaucratic ladders as they wish. Masoumeh Ebtekar, Deputy President under President-elect Khatami, known in the West as the spokesperson of the students during the American Embassy confrontation in Tehran, authenticates such claims. 'Muslim women' in Iran no longer appear to be deprived of any public activities; they have *their own* schools and universities, *their own* libraries, *their own* movie theatres, *their own* women's organizations, even their own fashion shows and horse-jumping competitions in which exotic, black-chadored 'female Zorros' participate energetically. Finally, 'Muslim women' have even established *their own* international Muslim women's conferences and regional annual sports games – which Iran has had to host year after year for lack of enthusiasm from other Islamic countries. All this attests to the claim that 'Islam' does not limit opportunities for women. Far from it. Islam, we are told, can provide an 'alternative liberating ideology for women', in place of an elitist feminism initiated in the West and rooted in colonialism, linked to secularism and a problematic modernity.

In this chapter I seek to draw attention to the context of the Islamization policies in Iran and their impacts on women. My aim is to establish several points: First, that while the gender politics of the Islamic Republic over the years since 1979 have developed in directions not conceivable immediately after the Revolution, these developments are not self-explanatory. Not only is the extent of favourable changes reported by the media and academic writings in the West highly exaggerated, but the complicated and multi-faceted nature of the forces promoting change are not interrogated. Second, the favourable changes, small as they are, came about under the pressure of the tangible and earthly social, economic, political and cultural contradictions and conflicts, including secular women's remarkable resistance against Islamization policies. Finally, these realities, rather than providing evidence that 'Islam' is compatible with gender equity and the notion and reality of women's rights – in effect, banalizing fundamentalism and coyly presenting it as a new revolutionary project and a viable alternative to modernism – demonstrate that Islamic fundamentalism in the face of hard realities has no alternative but to compromise its utopia. The experience of women in today's Iran attests to the potency of forces of modernism in imposing retreats on one of the most resistant and reactionary Islamic regimes. No matter how distorted these forces, once in action they cannot be stopped. More than anything else, the remarkable resilience of Iranian women and the ingenious ways they have found to overcome gender barriers in 'Islamic' Iran establishes this reality. To twist this hard reality to fit the seemingly 'radical', anti-representational analyses in celebration of 'local', home-grown responses and 'culturally different' solutions would not be in the interests of women's struggle against forces of oppression in Iran and the region.

## The Islamization Project

Almost three weeks into the Revolution, Ayatollah Khomeini's state-ment on the veil, ordering working women to cover up, came down on secular, unveiled women. The Ayatollah's aims were clear. Veiled women, the symbolic representation of Islamic order, signified the sovereignty of the Muslim community, umma, in Iran. The women who took to the streets in protest saw the Ayatollah's order as the betrayal of the women's cause by the Revolution and its leaders.

This was the beginning of the end. Iran was to become the bastion of 'the true Islam'. This was to be achieved through reinsti-tution of Shari'a in personal status laws, through the enforcement of Islamic moral codes, and by nullifying the social and legal changes of previous decades. Hence, the sexual segregation of public life, the curbing of women's access to education and employment and the 'de-womanizing' of certain professions. The hard-won achieve-ments of the previous decades in advancing women's legal and social status were now put under threat. By confining women, the funda-mentalists hoped to confine the forces of modernism. By seizing the domains which had been captured by women under the ancien régime, the Ayatollah and his associates aimed at seizing back the socio-cultural territory that, beginning with the secular reforms of Reza Shah in the 1930s, had been surrendered to Iran's modernization process.

At first, women's forceful demonstrations, protests, sit-ins and work stoppages made the Ayatollah and his regime retreat on veil-ing. But this was only temporary.[1] A year later, in the summer of 1980, when the Islamic regime had firmly established itself in power through intimidation and by silencing and brutal suppression of the opposition, women were forcefully pushed under the veil, from which they had been forcefully pulled out by a modernizing state some forty years earlier.[2] The compulsory reveiling of women was followed in quick order by an onslaught in all areas of women's personal, legal and social rights. The Family Protection Act was suspended; the legal marriage age for girls was lowered to thirteen, and later to nine; female judges were disqualified from the bench; technical and vocational schools were closed to girls; women were banned from certain fields of higher education, such as engineering, agriculture and mathematical science; and hundreds of female professionals, teachers and government employees were purged, pressured into early retirement or forced to quit their jobs. Combining legal rulings with clerical decrees, political statements and new government policies, aided by the iron fists of the Hezbollah, the Islamic state started its march towards the desecularization of the society. The ruling clerics' 'moral purification of society', by cleansing unveiled women of the evils of modern values and practices, aimed at protecting society from immoral temptations.

However, re-Islamization policies did not proceed as the fundamentalists had anticipated. Indeed, the ideological onslaught produced effects quite the opposite of what the clerics had hoped for. Rising to the challenge, women responded creatively to policies designed to enforce domesticity and male notions of 'Muslim womanhood'. Women's resistance centred, above all, on two areas where the fundamentalists' offensive had been concentrated: *hejab* and work outside home. It took determination, moral strength and sacrifice for women just to hold on to their jobs despite the harsh and despicable new measures in operation in the workplace. But the stronger the pressure, the more determined women became. The advent of female film-makers, television camerawomen, taxi drivers, even a women truck driver – professional and artistic activities not accessible to women before the Revolution – must be seen in this light. Likewise, *hejab*, the emblem of the 'Islamic Revolution' and the most reassuring sign of the cleric's grip on power, became the symbol of women's defiance and resistance. Inadequately veiled (*bad-hejab*) young middle-class women were humiliated, fined, arrested, tortured by lashing, or murdered[3] but women's non-compliance remained a haunting concern for the Islamic Republic.

The outbreak of war with Iraq in September 1980 produced contradictory influences on the state's gender politics and women's quest for their rights. War efforts silenced challenges to Khomeini's authority and gave the Islamic regime a new legitimacy and support, freezing open resistance, including resistance from secular women. Khomeini's repeated reference to the war as God-given and a blessing must be understood in this light. However, war, and, particularly,

the migration of hundreds of thousands of skilled workers and professionals, slowed the process of replacing women employees and
professionals with men. Massive war efforts forced the use of women's volunteer and paid labour. For political and military expediency, rigid Islamic rules and ideals surrounding female domesticity
and seclusion had to be relaxed.

By the end of war, the re-Islamization of gender relations and the
reshaping of women's rights according to a more rigid interpretation of the Shari'a faced serious obstacles, including pronounced
resistance by women and youth. Morality Police and bystanders
clashed in the streets of major cities over the arrest of violators of
the Islamic dress codes. Since the Ayatollah's death in 1988, policies
were aimed at confining and controlling demands for change. But
protests continued, and men of power became alarmed. Understanding 'anti-imperialism' as cultural war against Western values,
the ruling clerics were shaken by the defiance of 'women and youth',
by their disconcerting apathy towards 'Islamic' principles. A report
produced by the Social and Psychological Research Centre of the
President's Office, indicated that young people 'had become morally
vulnerable'; they showed 'defiance and disobedience', and 'linked all
political and social contradictions and shortcomings to religion'. A
new ideological onslaught was instigated to win back women and
youth.[4]

With the Ayatollah dead, re-Islamization policies were revisited
combining force with new efforts at persuasion. Shock troops for
Islamization regrouped, new 'Islamic' traditions were invented.
Modern concepts and practices were presented to society in 'Islamic'
wrapping. Hence, the celebration of Islamic Mothers' Day and
Women's Day and the extravagant celebration of Puberty (Jashn-e
Taklif) for nine-year-old girls, who, according to Shari'a, reach
womanhood at nine and can be married off. An extensive programme
of indoctrination and resocialization, aimed at creating a new value
system and achieving compromises in areas that had caused frustration to youth, was implemented to save the Revolution and its 'Islamic
values'. These efforts included contradictory practices – offering music
lessons and video clubs in neighbourhood mosques and, at the same
time, enforcing segregation by sex in all places in which the sexes

came into contact, even including Tehran buses. Enforcing Islamic morality entailed drastic interference in the privacy of the individual such as declaring the appropriate hair-cut for youth.

To aid political and cultural resocialization, the school curriculum was restructured to include courses on Islamic morality at every level, from kindergarten to the university – a policy which had started immediately after the Revolution. Now every field of higher education, from the humanities and social sciences to mathematics and medicine, included courses on Islamic principles and morality. Elementary and high-school textbooks were rewritten to accord with the official gender line. In school books the presence of female characters was reduced and refocused, emphasizing women's wifely and motherly roles and their domestic responsibilities (Mehran, 1991). A schoolchildren's annual Competition for Citation of the Qur'an was introduced. Female militia (*basiji*) were organized in schools to oversee compliance with the Islamic code.[5]

Re-Islamization and resocialization led to a proliferation of female-centred offices, committees and commissions within the state bureaucracy, such as the Bureau for Women's Affairs, the Women's Cultural and Social Council, the Women's Commissions in the Ministry of Internal Affairs and the Women's Bureau of International Propaganda in the Ministry of Foreign Affairs. Various groups nominally 'non-governmental' were funded by the state, including the Society of Women of the Islamic Republic and the Women's Section of the Society for Islamic Propaganda (*Howzeh-ye Tablighat-e Eslami*). To carry the torch, a group of trusted Muslim women were recruited from the homes of powerful clergymen, such as the daughter and the daughter-in-law of Ayatollah Khomeini, and the daughters of Ayatollah Yazdi (the Chief Justice), the deceased Ayatollah Dastghaib, Ayatollah Khazali (member of the powerful Guardianship Council) and President Rafsanjani. To these were added widows or mothers of Martyrs of the Revolution, such as the deputy Maryam Behroozi, former deputy Aateghe Rajaii and Nafiseh Fayyazbakhsh. This group would present a new role model for Iranian women, reshaping consciousness to favour the status quo.

What is the meaning of these state-initiated changes for women? Through an analysis of two areas of women's lives – women's rights in the family, including the provisions of the Qisas (Law of Retribution), and work outside the home – which have occasioned optimistic, even exuberant, analyses of women's status in Iran, I will try to demonstrate the paradoxical character of the fundamentalists' gender politics and how the careless interpretations or even outright misrepresentation of objective facts obscures these paradoxes.

## Women's Legal Rights in the Family

The new divorce law (Family Law) enacted by the Islamic regime in Iran is an area often represented as a major achievement for women under Islamic rule. This requires a closer examination. Our review of factors involved in the law's enactment should uncover the masterful manipulation of observers[6] by the fundamentalists, as well as the limits (and possibilities) of reforms within the Islamic framework. Does the new Family Law herald a breakthrough for women's rights in Iran? Timid and ineffectual, it demonstrates, instead, the impossibility of effecting meaningful change in women's status within the confines of the Islamic Shari'a.

After the Shah's downfall, one of the first 'revolutionary' decisions made by Ayatollah Khomeini was the abolition of the Family Protection Act (FPA).[7] The FPA was passed by the parliament (Majlis) in 1967, after years of campaigning by Iranian feminists, long hesitation by the state and heated debates. One of its highlights, which caused strong opposition from clergy at the time, dealt with divorce and child custody. Despite a proposal by the Association of Women Lawyers, the FPA did not annul the most discriminatory articles of the Civil Code taken directly from the Shari'a. It did not include, for example, the prohibition of polygamy and temporary marriage; nor did it provide for women's equal rights in divorce, custody and the guardianship of children; nor did it ensure women's equality of rights in inheritance or women's rights, after divorce, to sustenance and women's right to work outside the home – all of which would have represented a break from the Shari'a on the most important issues of women's personal status. The draft passed by the Majlis tried to modify, in women's favour, some of the provisions of the Civil Code, particularly Article 1133, which gives the husband a unilateral right to divorce by ruling that a 'man can divorce his wife if and when he so wishes'. The aim of the FPA, so cautiously advanced, was to provide some elementary protection to women without removing men's authority and prerogatives. Under the FPA, for example, the custody of children, previously a non-negotiable right of the father for boys over two and girls over seven, was made conditional on the decision of the Family Courts. By bringing some elements of family practice within the control of the state, arbitrariness would be reduced.

Even these modest reforms infuriated the Muslim clergy, particularly Khomeini, who condemned the Act as a ploy of foreigners and the government to interfere with the explicit words of God and 'the sacred Islamic texts.'[8] Suspension of the Family Protection Act after 1979 negatively affected women of all classes, particularly poorer women, as was first picked up by secular feminists and left and liberal women's organizations active immediately after the Revolution. In a couple of years, however, when the devastating consequences of the Ayatollah's decision could no longer be ignored, the Muslim female elites became more vocal on the subject. Particularly after the Ayatollah's death, they and the state-sponsored women's journals started a campaign for fairer family legislation. They focused on the destructive results of men's unrestricted and unconditional legal rights over women and reported on specific cases. The activities of the Muslim female elite were animated by the influx of individual complaints; by sit-ins in the houses of grand ayatollahs[9] by women widowed in the war with Iraq, who under *Shari'a* were denied custody of their children; and by reports on the skyrocketing rate of divorce (up to 200% in Tehran in only one decade), as discussed in the *Majlis*.[10] The role of the Martyrs' Foundation on behalf of young widows who had lost their husbands in the Iran–Iraq war as well in pushing for an amendment to the Family Law is noteworthy.[11]

Alarming as well was the steep increase in this period in the number of violent crimes committed against women by their husbands, further reducing women's sense of security and self-worth. Many of these crimes were known to have been committed by men who wanted to get rid of their wives with the intention of remarriage. Suicides also increased, and news media reported the self-burning of young mothers in Tehran, as well as in remote villages and provincial towns.[12]

Despite these alarming reports, political pressure, and the imperative practical need for reformed legislation, the enactment of a new family law did not materialize during the Ayatollah's lifetime. The new law was only passed in 1992, amidst much rhetorical excitement on the part of state officials about changes now pending in women's familial rights under Islamic rule. This enthusiasm was immediately taken up by a number of female academics living outside Iran, the majority of whom, in their writings at least, took the legislation and the words of the clerics at face value.

The new Islamic legislation has been presented as a law 'which Muslim women activists lobbied for, and Ayatollah Khomeini signed in 1987'; it is also claimed that the law 'offers women more actual protection than had been afforded by the Shah's Family Code' (Hoodfar, 1993: 12). Both these assertions are not true. The Ayatollah never signed the reformed family law. Its final version was ratified by the Expediency Council (*Shuray-e Maslahat-e Nezam*) in 1992, several years after Khomeini's death, and only after years of being batted back and forth between the *Majlis* and the Guardianship Council (*Shuray-e Negahban*)[13] which checks with the Islamic *Shari'a* for the consistency of all the legislation ratified by the *Majlis*. Moreover, as I will shortly discuss, the new legislation is far behind the FPA passed under the Shah, particularly on the questions of divorce and child custody.

In the congratulatory reports on the new law hardly any mention is made of the social and economic problems which instigated the change, including the deteriorating situation of women after the annulment of the FPA. Credit is given instead to the initiatives of 'Muslim female activists' and to the good will of Iran's clerical rulers. For example, Parvin Paidar, among others, presents the enactment of the law as the outcome of efforts by an increasingly autonomous and independent 'Islamic feminist opposition'. Thanks to the 'maturing effects' following the early post-revolutionary 'extremist years', these Islamic feminists changed their positions and moved towards a more moderate and 'autonomous existence' (Paidar, 1996: 62). According to Paidar, '[i]t took forty years for secular feminists of the Pahlavi era to change the family law.... In 1979, it took Ayatollah Khomeini one speech to demolish the Family Protection Law in a single blast; and since then it has taken Islamic feminists over twelve years to build it again bit by bit' (Paidar, 1996: 63–4). On this account, the (partial) reinstating of the Shah's Family Protection Act (FPA) was the result of the 'Islamic feminist opposition', and not of the combination of diverse factors and exigencies – the deep social crisis – mentioned earlier. Furthermore, in this version, all women in parliament and public institutions who lobbied for family law reforms are conveniently labelled as 'feminists' – and feminists who, moreover, assert their autonomous determination within an Islamic framework.

The re-enactment of a family law is, undoubtedly, one step forward among the many steps taken backward after the Revolution. But one should not exaggerate. With its hesitation and wavering, the Islamic family law represents the limits of the reform that is achievable within an Islamic framework. It shows, as nothing else, the stubborn and, indeed, self-defeating resistance of the clerics in an area that most desperately requires challenge, that is, in women's rights (or the lack of it) in the family. Closer examination of two issues, child custody and divorce, illuminates the extent to which reform has been circumscribed by conservative clergy in the Guardianship Council.

Like the pre-revolutionary Family Protection Act (FPA), Iran's recently enacted Islamic family legislation makes divorce subject to court approval, with each partner having the right, nominally, to institute proceedings; and it is the court, finally, which issues the decree. In cases, however, where the court finds the husband's decision to divorce his wife to be *'unjustified and without acceptable excuse'* (my emphasis), the husband is required to pay his wife for her accumulated unpaid labour in the matrimonial home. Still, the divorce is granted. In effect, as Mehrangiz Kar, a practising lawyer in Iran, notes, this reinstitutes the man's unilateral right to divorce, which the FPA had annulled; for the man has the last word.[14] He can decide to divorce his wife, regardless of her wishes; and even if his reasons are 'unjustified', the court must rule in his favour. Indeed, Kar declares that *not even once* in her experience as a lawyer has she seen an Iranian court deny a man's request for divorce. Moreover, under the new law, a divorced woman is not entitled to alimony beyond the three months and ten days waiting period (*eddeh*) that she must observe before being able to remarry.[15] If the woman proves that she did not mean to donate (*hebeh*) her matrimonial labour, the new law makes her ex-husband pay for it. It is up to the presiding judge. It goes without saying that such a condition makes the decision over payment, and over the possibility of divorce generally, extremely discretionary – wearying in its legal complications and conditional, in the end, on the personal, moral and religious values of the individual judge.

Another area where the new legislation is less woman-friendly by far than the FPA regards the questions of polygamy and temporary marriage, *mut'a*.[16] The 1975 law tried to limit polygamy by making it conditional on the first wife's permission. The man's remarriage was also one of the grounds that entitled the first wife to institute divorce proceedings (Afkhami, 1994: 351–60). By contrast, the new law keeps silent about polygamy and temporary marriage, and in so doing, actually encourages these practices. In addition, *mut'a* is encouraged through the creation of cleric-run Marriage Institutions, especially designed to facilitate the practice. These institutions help foster the outrageous conception of women as disposable commodities which can be used and then discarded, after consumption. The consequence for poor women in rural areas has been devastating. For example, a report by the General Director of Imam Khomeini's Aid Committees (*Komitehay-e Emdad-e Emam Khomeini*), describes the thousands of girls from poor families who were sold in Khorasan province for a cheap price, and the many more thousands who were 'married off' to Afghan refugees, without proper registration and were then deserted by their 'husbands' in and around Mashhad and the border with Afghanistan.[17]

The new legislation is also much behind the FPA on the right of women to custody of their children (*hezanat*). Even if *hezanat* is granted to a woman at the time of divorce or because of the death of her husband, this right does not include guardianship (*velayat*). Guardianship is the non-negotiable right of the father and of the paternal grandfather in case of the father's death. This also was a regression from the Family Protection Act, as amended in 1975, granting women the guardianship of their children. In fact, the unconditional rights of fathers to the custody of their children has always been one of the major concerns of Iranian women. Law gives the guardian (father) the right to treat the child any way he see fit and the scope of such authority is very broad under the Islamic criminal law (Qisas). A father or the paternal grandfather are not punishable by the law if they kill the child under their guardianship (Article 220). Literally, they have the right of life and death over their children. It is also noteworthy that a woman's claim under *hezanat* would collide with the reduced marriage age of nine for girls and fifteen for boys, and the right of the guardian (*vali*) to marry off the child under his custody even before she reaches the Islamified legal marriage age (Article 1210 of the Civil Code). The official statistics on marriage in Iran make it clear that child marriage is not as rare as assumed. In 1993, 741 of a total 4792 women reporting marriage (over 15%) were between nine and fourteen years of age.[18] Added to this is the alarming increase in reports of child abuse in the hands of fathers and step-mothers in Iran.[19]

If regressive legislation such as temporary marriage (*mut'a*), the restoration of the man's right to exclusive guardianship (*velayat*), and the punitive freedom afforded by the Qisas are taken into account, the horrifying consequences of two decades of fundamentalist rule in Iran can be more clearly appreciated.

## The Law of Retribution

The provisions of the Qisas (Law of Retribution) in Iran solidify gender inequality and have actually boosted violence against women.[20] To be sure, the archaic provisions of the law and the barbaric form of prescribed punishment (including stoning to death) violates the basic human rights of both sexes. But the law is clearly, unapologetically, harsher on women. Consider, for example, that the age of criminal responsibility – *masouliat jazaii* – is nine for girls and fifteen for boys; that the law only punishes women for their defiance of the dress code, *Hejab Sharii* (Article 639); that in stoning to death the procedures laid down for this horrifically barbaric practice are harsher for women. For in the process of stoning, men are to be buried up to their waist and women up to their chest (Article 102). Obviously, the possibility of escaping the punishment by freeing oneself from the hole (Article 103) is greater for a man than for a woman. In addition, the blood money (dieh) payable to the family of the victim for the death of a man is twice that for a woman (Article 258). This means that in Islamic Iran a woman's life (calculated in financial terms) is officially cheaper than a man's. This provision, in fact, has caused an unprecedented increase in violence against women. As admitted by Chief Justice Ayatollah Yazdi, it has encouraged the murder of women under the pretext of defending 'family honour'. 'Many women and girls live in constant fear for their lives' simply because, as stated by the Chief Justice, 'some men murder their wives or daughter on slight suspicion and then are easily set free by paying a very low sum of compensation [blood] money [dieh].'[21] These murders have caused so much concern, particularly in the southern province of Khuzistan, that the Chief Justice has had to instruct the courts not to free murderers without a proper investigation. But he is not prepared to admit that this situation cannot be blamed only on the deviant character of the men who resort to these crimes. It is part and parcel of a value system, promoted by the fundamentalists, which sees women and their bodies as possessions of men. On this view, purification of the woman's body and soul is a religious and political duty for the individual man, and through him, by extension, for the Islamic state. By the same token, when moral rules are perceived to have been broken, the man has the obligation (and therefore the justification) to punish the rule-breaker. The violent solution is bound up in the fundamental inequality assumed and enforced between women and men.

Setting a higher price on a man's life also means that rape and women's murder go unpunished. Under the Iranian criminal code these crimes are punishable by death. But under the new, 'Islamified' law, the family of a murdered woman is required to pay a substantial sum of dieh to the murderer before he can be punished (Article 209). In the words of Said Zadeh, a reform-minded cleric and advocate of Islamic justice for women, Article 209 values the murdered female less than her male murderer. If the family of the victim cannot come up with *dieh*, the murderer goes unpunished.[22]

It should go without saying that the social and cultural consequences of this legislation go beyond its impact on individuals. By cheapening the price of a woman's life, Article 209 proves that in Iran, today, full citizenship remains a male prerogative. In fact, laws like these constitute an assault on the dignity of women; they negatively affect social perceptions about women and women's own sense of self-worth and confidence, forcing them to live under constant fear. Fear is a dangerously potent instrument in cementing men's power to make it look unbeatable and to coerce women into submission.

## Paid Work as a Terrain of Contestation

An alleged 'increase' in women's employment in the public domain is a point constantly reiterated in recent academic writings on women in Iran, taking this as a sign of the regime's self-transformative capacity and the 'success' of Muslim women activists in pushing for change even within the strict limits of the Islamic regime. The analysis of women's employment is based on officially published data, including the Census. Comparing pre-and post-revolutionary figures, the conclusion is drawn that women's employment has increased under the Islamic government.

However, these analyses stubbornly insist on women's *increased* access to employment opportunities when all government statistics illustrate the opposite, and when the opposite view is also confirmed even by leading state officials, including the Chief Justice, Ayatollah Yazdi, and Zahra Shojaii, the Head of the Women's Cultural and Social Council (*Showra-ye Farhangi Va Ejtema'i-e Banavan*).[23] With the exception of Haleh Afshar (1997), whose research on women's employment results in different conclusions, the reference point for almost all of the optimistic feminist scholars who claim an increase in women's employment in post-revolutionary Iran is a single article by Valentine Moghadam (1988). A discussion of the major premises and claims put forward in this piece will help explain the basis for many of the misconceptions and errors about women's paid work in Iran in the post-revolutionary period.

In her study of women's employment, Moghadam, by comparing the results of the 1976 Census (the last before the Revolution) with the 1982 annual random data, concludes that 'women actually make up a slightly higher proportion of the work force than they did in 1976'. For several reasons, this is an erroneous claim. First, of the seven-year span between 1976 and 1982 used by Moghadam, at least three years are those of the pre-revolutionary period, and since Moghadam does not use annual time series data, the comparison of two cross-sections cannot show how much of this 'higher proportion' relates to changes recorded in the last period under the Shah, and how much of the overall change is accounted for by an increase in the post-revolutionary period.[24] Second, the Census data of 1986 (the first after the Revolution) totally contradict the author's conclusion, and show a decline in overall employment. This is despite the inflating effects of explosive population growth in the post-revolutionary period. Moreover, the Islamic Republic decreased the age category of employment from ten (used in pre-revolutionary censuses) and included seasonally unemployed individuals in the 'employed' category. Thus, the overall employment figures in the post-revolutionary census are inflated. Yet despite these changes in statistical concepts a more careful reading of Census data shows a substantial decline in the absolute number of females employed after the Revolution. The share of economically active women in the total economically active population decreased from 14.8% in 1976 to 10.2% in 1986. Moreover, the share of the employed urban female population in the total employed urban population decreased from 11.2% to 8.8% in the same period, and the female share of unemployed in urban areas increased from 13.1% in 1976 to 20.1% in 1986 (Iran Statistics Centre, 1375/1990: 58, 59).

The average rate of growth of women's employment in large industries (employment settings with ten employees or more and a strategic sector for women's employment) was reduced to an average of 4.3% from 7.0% in 1976. In the industrial sector where Moghadam believes she has detected 'a sharp decline in female factory employment', the author erroneously compares the 1976 Census data on 'women earning wages and salaries in the public and private sector [making] up between 20 and 27 percent' with the 1983 data of 'female wage and salary earners in urban factory employment [which] … represent 6 percent of total employment here' (Moghadam, 1988: 233; italics added). In other words, her data relate to two different types of industrial groupings. In 1976, the data are given for all industries, urban and rural, small and large, with one employee or more. In 1983, the data are given for 'large industries' (which the author calls urban industries) with at least ten employees. The author's 'sharp decline' reflects this statistical error, as 20% for the former category is compared with 6% for the latter.

Moghadam then explains the 'sharp decline' by arguing that 'most of these women were employed by multinational corporations (MNCs)', and that when these firms 'closed down or changed owners, preferential treatment in hiring practices was accorded to men.' This is also a mistake. First, the claimed change in the female employment ratio (from about 20% to 6%), as mentioned above, relates to the inclusion for 1976 data of small industries (fewer than ten employees), with which the MNCs in Iran (as everywhere else) had no connection. Second, all the MNCs in Iran under the Shah were joint ventures between the government and the private sector, in which foreign owners held a minority share. After the Revolution, these joint ventures came under government control. Their employment policies were no different from other government-owned and nationalized industries (Rahnema, 1990: 296).

The reality is that although the Census data of 1986 show some decline in the overall female employment, the number of female workers in 'large' industries has actually increased (Iran Statistics Centre, 1363/1984). The reason is quite simple. The Islamic Republic has never had any problem with the use of cheap female labour in Iranian industries. In a later article on the subject, written to 'update' her previous work on female employment in Iran, Moghadam repeats the same errors and adds to them. Using 1986 Census data which probably were not available to her at the time of writing her previous piece allows her to refer to the correct ratio of female employment and its *decline* (my emphasis), but without explaining or correcting her previous claims. She then attributes the decline to, among other things, the lack of inclusion of or not 'adequately count[ing] cottage industries in 1986' (Moghadam, 1995: 180). The puzzled reader wonders on what basis this claim is made. Why would the Islamic Republic's all-encompassing Census not include the data for hundreds of thousands of cottage industries, while (as was mentioned earlier) it counts workers six years old and above (as opposed to ten years old and above in the pre-revolutionary Census) as well as the seasonally employed within the 'employed' category?

As for the growth of female employment in the public sector under the Islamic government, Moghadam is right in her assessment, although again she does not specify what portion of the increase is related to the pre-revolutionary period (1976–79). Neither does she adequately explain various factors which boosted the number of female public-sector employees. These include the rapid population growth after the Revolution, itself partly the result of the earlier policies of the Islamic Republic which dramatically increased the number of elementary students, and, consequently, the need for teachers. Teachers constitute the largest segment (over 70%) of female employment in the public sector. In addition, political expediency – the employment of large numbers of female family members of government officials, the martyrs (*shohada*), the veterans (*janbazan*), and the war disabled (*ma'lulin*) – has also promoted women's employment. But the author implies that this growth has been the result of the 'maturity' of the Islamic government and its ideological transformation.

In another article, Moghadam alludes to the increased social roles for women in Iran, including their military training. She states that women are assigned the responsibility to 'guard government ministries and banks', and asserts that '[e]ntrusting women with such public responsibility is contradictory to the earlier decisions of the Islamic Republic to remove women from the ranks of public officialdom' (Moghadam, 1991: 280). Most of the women to whom she refers are employed in coercive apparatuses designed to control and police other women in public institutions; their employment is not contradictory to the early policies of the Islamic state. Here again, blindness to the ideological aspect of the state's employment and educational policy leads to a one-sided appreciation of new developments in these areas. After the Revolution, women were recruited into such institutions as the all-female morality squads, Islamic Associations of government and semi-government agencies, the Pasdaran Corps, the Society for Islamic Propaganda, the Martyr's Foundation (Bonyaad-e Shahid) and the militia,[25] and the special women's committees in neighbourhood mosques – all charged with the mandate to disseminate Islamic values through indoctrination and intimidation. Those of us who worked in public institutions after the Revolution know only too well that body-searching, removing make-up and perfume from female employees and clients, and overseeing compliance to fundamentalists' moral codes constituted these women's main responsibility. Their employment at such tasks hardly constitutes entry into 'public officialdom'.[26]

Two points are of particular importance in the study of women's employment in post-Revolution Iran. First, the state's policies in this area and their impact on women cannot be analysed in isolation from the long-term goals of the Islamization project. At the top of the agenda is sexual apartheid in the production and use of knowledge. The fundamentalists hope to channel women's professional and paid activities towards occupations where women predominate and whose value, in consequence, is taken to be less. Intimately joined to this project is the use of educational institutions and the state bureaucracy to promote Islamic moral values and ideological concerns. For instance, the number of female entrants to medical schools increased sharply in the post-war period. Women came to constitute 50% of the students enrolled in medicine. Partly, this increase reflects the expansion of medical schools and the creation of new ones, more than trebling the number of schools from eight (in 1978) to thirty (in 1992).[27] In the same period, despite the massive exodus of full-time faculty after the Revolution, the number of medical students multiplied sixfold from 5,000 to 32,000. Yet women's concentration in obstetrics/gynaecology (now closed to male students), pediatrics, and family medicine, and women's virtual exclusion from medicine's technical frontiers such as neurology[28] demonstrate again the ideologization of female education and employment, and the unremitting commitment to segregation in the workforce. This policy culminated in the enactment of a law in October 1998, requiring the sexual segregation of health care services at all levels according to the *Shari'a* rules.

The formation of the Unit of Sisters' Affairs (*Vahed-e Omour-e Khaharan*) in the much publicized Islamic Open University (*Daneshgah-e Azad-e eslami*) is one example of how female-centred institutions and offices serve the gender politics of the state, rather than promoting higher education for women. The Unit has representatives in 110 campuses established by the Open University. The goal of advancing the cause of women's education does not seem to be a priority for the Unit. Among its major responsibilities are 'to present the Islamic role model to female students and to establish marriage centres [*kanoon-e ezdevaj*] for girls and boys who cannot find suitable partners to marry'.[29]

This is not to deny that in the long run the increase in women's public presence in the schools and workforce will benefit women. But these advances, selective as they are, are deeply beset by contradictions, paradoxes and complications which became even more tenacious after 1988. Despite its holy war against secular values, clerical gender politics pertaining to women embody unplanned and unsought-for gains which are favourable to women. Even the mere presence of 'working' women in the state bureaucracy, educational institutions and industry can represent, perhaps, a partial defeat for the fundamentalists, who hoped for the establishment of a gendered Islamic law and order through an absolute de-womanization of public life. Perhaps in studying women's employment in post-revolutionary Iran, what is most important is why the female employment ratio has not declined any further, or why all working women could not be returned, as is the case, for example, under the Taliban in Afghanistan. The hard rock struck by the Islamic Republic is that it is dealing with women's status in a society with a relatively advanced level of capitalist development. We need to understand the clearly observable paradoxes of the Revolution to appreciate what the Islamic state was facing. True, modernization in the manner followed under the Shah disenchanted the Iranian people and helped instigate the revolution which brought the clergy to power. But even tasting the impact of modernization blocked the implementation of the ruling clergy's agenda, obstructing their efforts to establish a utopian Islamic order. Decades of capitalist development, industrialization, consumerism, and the associated impacts of the market economy, have irreversibly altered the lives of many women, and have introduced inevitably a more relaxed gender interaction. These changes can be lamented, assaulted, outlawed, prohibited; but they cannot be undone.

The economic and social changes in the pre-revolutionary period provided many women, including women from the lower-middle classes, with access to education and, increasingly, to some forms of paid work. The younger generation, growing up under Islamic rule, expect the same. Economic conditions are even more compelling than women's aspirations. The Islamists could hope for the replacement of secular women with trusted, practising Muslims, ideologically 'transformed' women, or women who simply managed to pass the formal ideological tests necessary for entry into university or government employment. But 'cleansing' the public sphere and state institutions by expelling women and returning them to their homes is no longer a credible goal.

In all this the question we come down to is why is it that the stagnation (or regression) in women's access to employment and education is not taken as a serious blow to women's status in a non-Western context such as Iran, as they would be had the authors been dealing with women's status in the West? Can this attitude be understood in any way other than as reflecting the *low expectations* of cultural relativists when it comes to the rights of women in non-Western societies?

## Resistance to the Islamization Project

None of what has been said, however, is to suggest that women have been the passive victims of the Islamization policies in Iran. To be sure, women since the Revolution have been at the forefront of the struggle to secure democracy for Iran. No other element of post-revolutionary politics could expose the cruel and archaic character of Islamic rule with greater clarity than its atavistic gender politics and its fruitless moral crusades against women. These have delegitimized the ruling clergy and disillusioned millions, women and men, who joined the revolution with great hopes for change.

Today in Iran, specific feminist ideas and many demands for legal equality, paid housework and shelters (*khanehay-e amn*), are gaining ground and are openly debated, albeit quietly and timidly. This marks a new step. Immediately after the Revolution, such ideas were frowned upon and dismissed as having no relevance. The Islamic state has also had to overlook the publication of several feminist journals, such as *Zanan, Payam-e Hajar* and *Farzaneh*, which do not trespass on Islamic boundaries. Feminist projects of this kind raise public awareness and challenge male-centred cultural and social values. They make women's presence in public more acceptable and draw attention to invisible gender discrimination in employment and education. However, all this, far from speaking to the compat-ibility of clerically defined Islam with a feminist agenda, testifies, instead, to the 'un-Islamic' character of the changes. Islam and Islamic rulers have not suddenly gone feminist. It is women and the hard realities of modern times which have imposed retreats on the clerical rulers and 'their' Islam.

How best to express solidarity with the quiet, determined struggle of Iranian women and how best to link it to struggles for dem-ocracy and basic human rights throughout the region is a most demanding challenge facing intellectuals, including feminists, in-side and outside Iran. This is a large 'how', still in the process of formation. But perhaps we can start by listening more carefully to the voices of women inside Iran, particularly voices of gender-conscious women who have generated all the excitement among academic feminists, but, themselves, have remained unenthused with changes in the last few years, without becoming discouraged or cynical.

Shahla Lahiji, a feminist publisher and author, for example, calls upon her sisters outside the country 'not to get too exhilarated and excited about what is happening in Iran. Do not consider as a movement or a revolt what we consider there just as a wave', she says; and 'do not get bewitched with a few developments.' Addressing the question as to which groups of women have been more important in inducing change, Lahiji comments, 'We have a movement of individual women [*Monfared*].' The legal issues and social problems they discuss are picked up by women of the establishment and presented to society to gain social popularity.[30]

Likewise, Shirin Ebadi, a female lawyer, author and activist challenges those feminists who cheer the increased number of women in parliament or the appointment of a few chosen women to high-ranking administrative positions, arguing that 'women's problems [in Iran] are much deeper than their rights in the family or access to public office.' Ebadi believes that the appointment of a few to high office does not mean much if women in their generality are denied full citizenship status. Referring to the fact that women's lives are valued at half men's in the Islamic Republic, Ebadi argues: 'I should first acquire the right to life, to be recognized as a full human being, and then expect to have the right to compete for the presidency.'[31]

A similar position is offered by Mehrangiz Kar. A regular contributor to the journal, *Zanan*, Kar has repeatedly criticized the shortcomings of the new Islamic family law, stressing that it falls behind what was already achieved under the Shah.[32] Generally she urges restraint in new directions in feminist politics in Iran. For example, at a conference at the University of Southern California, Kar refused to accept the compliment made from the audience that *Zanan* represented 'a milestone' for Iranian feminists, saying, quite plainly, that this was probably not the case, and that 'we are simply trying [to do] our best, under present circumstances.' Kar distrusts the exuberance expressed about new developments in Iran, including the grand hopes which feminist scholars outside the country have pinned to the activities of the new 'Muslim feminists'.

In this context, I would argue that reports in the West of favourable developments for women under the Islamic Republic are quite naïve, to say the least. Many of these reports are produced with very good intentions – that is, to draw attention to the fact that when discussing fundamentalism in the Muslim world we should pay more attention to the dynamics of the relationship between the fundamentalists and women, between the 'text' and the 'context', and to what 'women do with fundamentalism or how fundamentalism works in practice' (Haeri, 1995: 131). This is sound advice. But only one side of the 'dynamic' excites the feminist imagination of the author: women's response to fundamentalism. What is comfortably overlooked here is 'how fundamentalism works in practice', and particularly, how its practices affect women's lives. Undoubtedly, women's resistance is a most remarkable aspect of 'the dynamics of the relationship between the fundamentalists and women'. But women's resistance should not be over-emphasized. The practical consequences of fundamentalism, particularly the hostile legal practices which circumscribe women's day-to-day experiences, should not be overlooked. The difference between 'text' and 'context', between what fundamentalists say or wish and what they do in practice, is not as great as some feminists suggest. Indeed, what the fundamentalists believe to be women's 'Islamic' rights and obligations have been put into practice in areas of central importance such as criminal law and family law. And what fundamentalists 'do to women' in recent Islamic enactments is much more than 'what women do to fundamentalists'.

Moreover, in any country, the crucial difference between the 'rhetoric' and 'practice' of Islamic fundamentalists (their 'text' and 'context', as it is put in some recent formulations) can be better understood if we understand that the context includes not only the local variant of Islamic speech, but the compelling, material conditions under which the fundamentalists have imposed their rules. Generally, the higher the level of society's economic and cultural advance – particularly, the more developed and flexible its governing institutions – the greater the difference between what fundamentalists preach and what they are able to practise, both before they take power and after they have that power in their hands. In Iran, for example, if Khomeini and his supporters had captured power in the early 1960s, when they first challenged the Shah and when the country was less secure, both economically and socially, the Republic would have been more successful in implementing its Islamization policies; the old regime's material incapacity and its traditional political narrowness and authoritarianism would have facilitated the imposition by the Islamists of an equally retrograde agenda on gender. But the takeover was delayed for nearly twenty years. However uneven and class-limited their effects, two decades of capitalist growth and economic modernization under the Shah spoiled the possibility, in 1979, of an unhindered transition to a thoroughly Islamic regime, instead troubling the new rulers with a developed resistance, including strong opposition by women.

After two decades of fundamentalist rule, Iranians urgently demand social change. They demand a lawful state and individual rights – knowing, at the same time, that this is impossible when fundamentalists claim to take instructions from God alone, and when all wisdom is supposed to be inscribed in holy texts. In Iran today, the Islamic project is nearing exhaustion, its capacity for creative change used up. Iranian women and men knew this when they voted for Khatami in the spring of 1997, hoping that he would facilitate the shift to a secular state. Charmed by 'difference' and secure from the bitter facts of the fundamentalist regime, outsiders do them a disservice by clinging to the illusion of an Islamic path.

## Notes

This chapter draws partly on my article in Persian, 'Feminism-e populisti va feminism-e eslami: Naqdi bar gerayesh-haye-no mohafezekaraneh' (Populist Feminism and 'Islamic Feminism': A Critique of Neo-conservative Tendencies in Iranian Feminism), *Kankash* (New York), No. 13 (Fall), 1997. The section on fundamentalist gender practices immediately after the Revolution draws on my 'Women and Fundamentalism in Iran', in R. Lentin (ed.), *Gender and Catastrophe*, Zed Books, London, 1997. Earlier versions of this chapter were presented in a symposium on Fundamentalism, Feminism and Civil Society in Iran, House of Cultures of the World, Berlin, February 1998.

1. For an account of the events following Ayatollah Khomeini's pronouncement on veiling, women's response to it and the position of various secular political parties on the issue, see Moghissi (1994: 107–58). See also Tabari and Yaganeh (1982)

2. For an illuminating account of political events in the first few months after the revolution see Rahnema and Nomani (1990).

3. In the summer of 1993, Bahareh Vejdani, a teenage girl, was shot dead by police in a telephone booth in Tehran for defying the *hejab* code. See *Iran Times*, 11 September 1993.

4. *Iran Times*, 7 November 1991.

5. *Iran Times*, 28 September 1993.

6. For example, recently there were cheering reports on the appointment of female judges to a court in Shahr Rey, near Tehran. The Islamic

government, conscious of its reputation of banning women from the bench, let the report stand. The news was repeatedly referred to as a proof of changes initiated by the ruling clergy to raise women's status. It took several months before the accuracy of the report was called into question. Recently, in a long article, Mehrangiz Kar, a female lawyer and advocate of women's rights in Iran, explained that the (re)appointment of female judges could be read as a positive step in the right direction of reinstating women's right to become judges, but women were not actually returning to the bench yet. Kar made two further points: first, that the new ruling applies only to female judges who lost their positions after the Revolution and not to other women; secondly, these women will regain their position in courts but can only serve as *investigating judges*, under the instruction and supervision of *male judges* (Zanan, 40, 1998: 18–21).

7. On the FPA, see Bagley (1971).

8. For Ayatollah Khomeini's views on the FPA, see Ministry of Culture and Islamic Guidance (1366/1987: 133, 169–70).

9. For example, a young woman friend who spent four years in prison and whose husband was executed for 'counter-revolutionary' activities confronted the resistance of her father-in-law in seeking custody for her five-year-old son when she was released from prison in 1984. After she exhausted all avenues to gain custody of her child, she and her mother participated in several sit-ins at the house of the Grand Ayatollah Montazeri. She only won custody (and the possession of her apartment, which the father-in-law had also claimed) when her father-in-law yielded to pressures from relatives and friends.

10. Zan-e Rooz, 15 December 1989.

11. See interview with Mehrangiz Kar in Middle East Report, Vol 26, No. 198 (January–March) 1996.

12. Zan-e Rooz, 8 December 1991.

13. According to the Constitution of the Islamic Republic, all laws passed by parliament must be ratified by a twelve-member religious body called the Guardianship Council. Later Khomeini introduced yet another decision-making body, the Expediency Council (EC), which consists of selected representatives of the Parliament, the GC, the executive and judiciary branches. The EC must provide a final decision on issues in dispute between other bodies. Rafsanjani, the former president, managed to get himself appointed as Head of the EC after the 1997 election of Muhammad Khatami to the presidency.

14. Since the enactment of the new legislation, Mehrangiz Kar has repeatedly referred to the pre-revolutionary Family Protection Act as a well-considered piece of legislation which strengthened the family by placing the authority over divorce proceedings under state supervision. She insists that the FPA should be identified not as a property of the previous regime, but as something belonging to the nation. See Zanan, Aban 1374/October 1995: 16–21.

15. Zan-e Rooz, 18 Aban 1371/28 November 1992.

16. On the institution of mut'a see Chapter 1, n. 2.

17. Iran Times, 4 January 1993.

18. See Avay-e zan, Nos. 31–2 (Winter/Spring) 1998.

19. A particularly gruesome murder case which recently shocked Iran involved a twelve-year-old girl, Aryan, who was tortured and beaten to death by her father and step-brother. The mother's repeated pleas to the court to grant her Aryan's custody had been rejected. The judge told Aryan's mother that a father has the right to treat his daughter as he wishes and she had no right to interfere. See Zanan, Azar 1376/December 1997: 26–31. Several sensational reports on similar cases of child abuse forced the enactment of an amendment to the custody law. The amendment allows the court to give custody right to the mother provided that she proves that the father lacks competence (salahiat). Avay-e Zan, 1998: 7.

20. See the Islamic criminal law, Qisas (Ashrafi, 1375/1996: Articles 638, 639).

21. Zan-e Rooz, 12 Tir 1371/3 July 1993.

22. See S.M. Said-Zadeh, Zanan, Azar 1376/December 1998. Several recent rape–murder cases in Iran have caused much commotion and open criticism. In one case, the death penalty for two men who raped an eleven–year-old girl and cut her into pieces was not carried out because the girl's father has been unable to provide the blood money even after he sold his house (Zanan, Tir 1375/July 1996).

23. See, for example, Payam-e Hajar, 24 Tir 1372/6 August 1993 and Iran Times, 7 March 1991.

24. For example, in the education sector, one of the most important domains of women's employment, the percentage increase in employment for 1976–7, 1977–8, and 1978–9 were 11–12%, 12–13%, and 13–16% respectively. In 'large industries' (with ten employees and over), another major domain of women's employment, the average rate of growth in employment in 1976 was about 7%, and although this rate decreased from 6% to 2% in 1977, it again increased from 4% to 9% in 1978. However, between 1979 and 1982 (the post-revolutionary years), this rate dropped from 4% to 3%. The employment indices of these industries (base year 1974) for the years 1976, 1977, 1978 and 1979 were 117/3, 120/4, 126/3 and 132/8 respectively. See Bank-e Markazi-ye Iran/Central Bank of Iran (1364/1985: 174, 226, 571, 599).

25. By 1994 over 300,000 militia were recruited to push back the 'West's cultural invasion' and 300,000 more were to be hired as agents of ordering good and preventing evil (amr-e be marouf va nahy-e az monkar). See Iran Times, 28 October 1993.

26. For example, between 1980 and 1984, before my forced departure from Iran, the number of employees in the institution where I worked had increased significantly. Among the new intake were several women in black chador, including sisters of two shahid (martyrs) and two Iraqi Shi'is of Iranian origin who had been expelled from Iraq after the outbreak of the war. Some of these women were in charge of the body search operation at the

entrance of the building. A major responsibility of others who joined the
'professional' staff was to attend mandatory praying at noon and take note
whether other female staff actually prayed or just came to the room, stayed
a few minutes and left, as was initially the practice. It would not be a
surprise if some of these watching and checking women later acquired the
status (and training) of the regular professional staff and were promoted to
supervisory positions.

27.  For a unique analysis of health care policy and the state of the medical schools in Iran, see Rastegar (1996: 222–3) Rastegar's analysis demonstrates that the Islamic government's policy of mass production of university
graduates in the field of health care has been carried out without much
regard for the quality of education. For example, a massive increase in the
number of medical students means a higher ratio of students to professors
and lower teaching quality; only half of the university faculty have doctoral
degrees. Iran's Minister of Health recently expressed concern over the low
quality of the graduated physicians, a large number of whom cannot find
employment.

28.  See Zan-e Rooz, 12 Shahrivar 1370/22 September 1991.

29.  See Zan-e Rooz, 3 Mehr 1373/13 October 1994.

30.  Women in Struggle, No. 8, September 1997: 8.

31.  Zanan, No. 34, Ordibehesht 1376/May 1997: 15.

32.  In the 1997 annual conference of the British Society for Middle East
Studies (BRISMES) at Oxford University, Mehrangiz Kar's comments about
the increased rate of polygamous marriages in Iran infuriated a young
Paris-based feminist whose position had been contradicted by Kar's remarks. She said that Kar's comments had no basis and that her 'field research' did not show such an increase. Without challenging the merits of
the woman's research, Mehrangiz Kar reminded her that she is a practising
lawyer in Iran, and her studies and writings on the subject are aided by
this fact.

# Chapter 7

# Islamic Feminism
# and its Discontents

Feminism in the 1990s has shown a new and refreshing willingness to engage in self-criticism. Attempts at all-encompassing theories and concepts and the earlier ideological commitment to universalizing the perspectives of what turned out to be a single, specific culture, class and 'race' have long lost their merit. Placing emphasis, instead, at least in theory, on including *all* women by accepting the multiplicity of each woman's identity and self-identification, feminists are now urged to respect difference, affirming the singularity of each woman's experience and struggle, and validating self-understanding and self-analysis. Today, feminism has grown large and includes many brands, both conservative and radical, religious and atheist, heterosexual and non-heterosexual, white and non-white, issue-oriented and holistic, individualistic and community-oriented; and feminists hail from the North and the South. So the question, whether we can affirm a new brand of feminism which is self-identified or identified by others as 'Islamic feminism', is rather superfluous.

Still, 'Islamic feminism' is not as self-explanatory as the term may suggest. Certainly, such a feminism would not be only about articulating women's experience in religious terms. In fact, the 'Islamic' in 'Islamic feminism' raises many questions. For instance, what kind of 'Islam' and what sorts of relations with it are presumed? Do we mean 'Islam' as a medium uniting women and supposed cosmic power, in response to personal, gender-specific needs, or does the term instead entail a prescribed set of ideas,

teachings, texts, as applied to women, indeed an entire pre-estab-
lished moral and legal order? 'Islamic feminism' is connected with
the question of the compatibility of feminism with Islamic teaching
and scripture, and the social and legal frameworks which have
evolved in Islamic societies. How could a religion which is based on
gender hierarchy be adopted as the framework for struggle for gender
democracy and women's equality with men? And if Islam and feminism are compatible, which one has to operate within the framework of the other?

It is important to bear in mind that there is no coherent, self-
identified and/or easily identifiable 'Islamic feminist' ideology and
movement operating within the boundaries of Islamic societies. Of
course the term has been the subject of much ideological, political
and theoretical debate. But as a concept and a marker for a specific
brand of feminism, Islamic feminism from the start was adopted
and pushed from outside Islamic societies; it was the work, chiefly,
of diasporic feminist academics and researchers of Muslim background living and working in the West. Which is to say, in Islamic
societies, the majority of gender-conscious women, believers and
non-believers alike, who, in one way or other, are active in the
women's rights struggle rarely choose to identify themselves or to
be identified by others as feminists, be it Islamic feminist or not.
In fact, these women, fighters for equity, do not apply the term
'feminist' to themselves, or ever consider 'feminist ideas' as applicable to the Middle East.

By this, I do not mean that because these women (and men, in
certain cases) do not place their discourses and political activities
within the feminist framework marked out in the West they should
not be considered feminist. Nor is it to suggest that feminism is an
alien idea and goal, imported from the West to the Middle East. If
feminism, at its core, is a political and intellectual project advocat-
ing equal gender rights and demanding women's access to public
life, then feminism (without the name) has always been crucial in
Islamic societies. The publication in the last two decades of a rapidly
expanding literature on women and the women's movements in the
Middle East and North Africa should make this abundantly clear.
That movements for women's emancipation have always existed in

the Middle East contradicts facile arguments about the alien character
of feminism in the region. Equally, it casts doubt on any argument
which presents Islamic conceptions as the only possible frame of
reference for feminism in the region.

The issues of women's status and rights, and their compatibility
or incompatibility with the dictates of the Islamic *Shari'a* seem to
have been central to debates among both secularists and conservatives
in many Middle Eastern societies. In several Middle Eastern societies,
intellectual and political struggles for women's rights go back to the
late nineteenth century, although women's entry into the public
sphere and organized movments did not emerge until the turn of
the century. Characteristic of a Middle Eastern and, perhaps, global
pattern, initially, almost the entire energy of these pioneering women
was focused on mobilizing women in support of nationalist, anti-
colonial movements; it was the only form of women's political
engagement and public appearance which the male elite endorsed.
By the end of World War I, women had gained confidence and an
autonomous voice through their participation in the national liberation struggle.

The role of the state in assisting women's struggles has been
more prominent in some Islamic societies than in others. In Turkey,
for example, the state's role was crucial because changing law and
public women's appearances were both bound up with the creation
of a secular regime; the first written family code in the Muslim
world was introduced in Turkey in 1917 (Kandiyoti, 1991: 42). In
Egypt and Iran, debates over women's rights started with male reformers such as Muhammad Abduh, Qasim Amin, Mirza Fath-Ali
Akhundzadeh and Mirza Aghakhan Kermani, but women's eloquent
voices against patriarchal traditions and practices have also been
recorded as early as the mid-nineteenth century. In hindsight one
can say that these expressions were feminist.

Among the first gender-conscious women in the region were
Tahereh Qurrat-ol 'Ayne (mid-1800s Iran), Nazira Zin al-Din
(1920s Lebanon) and Fatima Aliya Hanim (late 1800s Turkey). They
criticized misogynist interpretations of the Qur'an and the male-
serving fabrication of the *hadith*, and attacked the veil, sex segregation and the gender-based restrictions that had been imposed on

Muslim women. In the late nineteenth century, feminist novelists and writers in Turkey began publication. Fatima Aliya and Zeyneb Hanoum, two pioneering women, got engaged in debates on women's rights and Islam. Since the Islamic framework was the only avenue available for legislative reforms, Aliya and Hanoum's book, *Muslim Women* (1891) took up the task of proving that Islam was compatible with women's demand for change (Jayawardena, 1986: 28–29; Kandiyoti, 1991).

Tahereh Qurrat-ol 'Ayne, was a fervent Babi and learned theologian and leader in her faith, a public scholar and passionate orator. In mid-nineteenth-century Iran, she criticized, problematized and questioned Islam's prescribed gender roles. Qurrat-ol 'Ayne objected to all forms of women's confinement, including the separation between public and private and the sharp distinction made between male and female roles. In 1848, she publicly unveiled herself, shocking the public, including her own people. As Farzaneh Milani notes, the extraordinary character of this woman and the importance of her messages can be better appreciated if we consider that this was a time when education still was a male prerogative and that words and discourse fell into the public domain from which women were banned; a woman's quest for scholarly education and knowledge were considered to be signs of 'insanity, promiscuity and heresy'. Remarkably, Milani notes, Qurratol 'Ayne, who unveiled herself so many years ago, 'still lives such a veiled life in the memory of her own people' (Milani, 1992: 86, 94).[1]

In this same period, two other critiques of religious and cultural practices and beliefs were put forth by Bibi Khanum Astarabadi, in her pamphlet *Moayeb-ul Rejal* (The Statesmen's Folly), and by Taj-ol Saltaneh. Using what might be called a radical feminist and anti-patriarchal discourse, Bibi Khanum passionately blamed men for women's degraded status in the family and in social life, declaring that 'all the problems and chaos faced by Iran and by its women were men's doings' (Nateq, 1358/1980: 45–53). Similarly, Taj-ol Saltaneh spoke of the idle life of urban upper-class women who could not participate in productive economic activities; she criticized oppressive traditions and customs both for retarding Iran's development and for depriving women (Ettehadieh, 1361/1982).

Starting in the early twentieth century, women's periodicals and journals followed in the footsteps of these courageous women, waging an extensive campaign for women's rights. Between 1910 and 1930 more than twenty women's periodicals started publication in Iran. As I have stated elsewhere, in a country where the publication of newspapers did not have a long history the sheer number of pro-women's rights publications speaks to the existence of a relatively strong women's movement.[2]

Similarly, a striking history of women's participation in nationalist movements and in stirring ideas about women's rights and gender equality exists in Egypt, beginning with the writings of such remarkable women as Zainab al-Fawwaz and Aisha al-Taimuriyya in the mid-nineteenth century. Margot Badran's extensive research and her impressive works on feminism in Egypt demonstrate that feminist awareness in the country was indigenously rooted. She calls into question the view that feminism in Egypt began with men (such as Muhammad Abduh and Qasim Amin), or that it was and is exclusively Western, or that this feminism has been only upper class. Badran errs, in my view, in arguing that Egypt's feminist movement was unique in that the fight for change in the personal status law came from women themselves, without state assistance; a situation, she says, quite different from that which faced women in Iran and Turkey. After all, the incorporation of Egypt into the world market in the mid-nineteenth century and the economic and social changes of the period inaugurated favourable changes, including educational opportunities, at least for urban, upper-class women. These were 'state-instigated' reforms, to which Badran herself makes a reference. However, I agree with Badran that women in Egypt were pioneers of the feminist struggle not only in their own country but also throughout the region. Indeed, it was Egyptian women who, for example, initiated unveiling in the early twentieth century, beginning with Huda Shaarawi's and Saiza Nabarawi's removal of their veils at Cairo railway station after returning from an international feminist conference, and who declared 'women's determination to put a final end to sex segregation and female seclusion in the home' (Badran, 1993: 135). Egyptian women also began to call themselves feminists in 1923 with the formation of the Egyptian Feminist Union (EFU).[3]

It is also quite impressive that the pioneers for women's rights
in the Middle East valued inter-regional and international cooperation
among women and emphasized the universal character of patriarchy. For example, the organization of two congresses of Eastern
Women – the first hosted by Syrian women in 1930; the second, by
Iranian feminists in 1932 – brought women together from the Middle
East and South Asia. Both congresses issued demands for equal rights
for women in the family, the abolition of polygamy, compulsory
elementary education, the franchise for women, and equal pay for
equal work (Ostadmalek, 1367/1988: 112–24). It is troubling and
revealing that the new generation of Middle Eastern feminists are
still struggling for these rights under the same if not more hostile
conditions in societies which are much more developed, socially
and economically, than in the 1930s.

From this brief review, it is evident that feminism, in its broad
sense, is not a new development in the Middle East. Neither is the
the strategy of drawing upon the Qur'an and early Islamic prece-
dents as opposed to later conservative interpretations, nor the push
for legislation to improve women's legal and social status. The drive
for women's rights from within the Islamic frame is not an invention of present-day Islamic feminists. To legitimize their demands,
the overwhelming majority of the pioneers for women's rights,
whether practising Muslims, non-practising believers, or even non-
believers and covert atheists, were obliged to develop alternatives to
orthodox interpretations of the Qur'an and other Islamic texts. Both
secularists and Muslim modernists stressed that women's degraded
conditions were the result of a gender-biased misreading of the
Qur'an, not the text itself. Muslim reformers claimed that Islamic
rules were male-biased, and a culturally distorted intepretation of
the Qur'an. They argued that the Qur'an never meant men to be
superior to women, or to force the *hejab* on women which pre-
vented them from taking the same social roles as men. But many
advocated modern political, administrative, legal changes, including
separation of state and religion, economic development, the rule of
law and equality for women. Unlike Muslim reformers, the ultimate
goal of the secular reformers, however, was not to modify *Shari'a*,
but to do away with it altogether. Some suggested Islam was their

moral and spiritual guide. But they hoped to de-shari'atize their country's legal and political structures. Given the cultural and social constraints operating at the time, they chose what they saw as the 'lesser evil', opting for an improved Islam and refined Qur'anic interpretations. In this way, they hoped to overcome the resistance of conservatives, including Islamic clerics and jurists, who manipulated public sentiments to block change and to present modern values and practices as un-Islamic and anti-Qur'an.

Obviously, none of these activities were carried on under the banner of 'Islamic feminism'. No need was felt to highlight or emphasize the 'Islamic' character of the activities which were carried out for improving women's lot. Why, then, are these discourses now identified as 'Islamic feminism' and why are they put forward by some secular feminists as the only viable, indigenously rooted framework for women's liberation? To explore this question, we should consider certain social, economic and political developments which predate the rise to prominence of Islamism and Islamic fundamentalism.

First, the ascent of women's struggle for change in a newly energetic global movement, from the 1960s onward. This has been the result of the transformation of social life and gender roles in contemporary society. The adoption of capitalist growth strategies modelled on the West and policed by the IMF and other monetary institutions created new problems for women as well as generating new social awareness. Entry into paid labour and changing family dynamics sparked dissatisfaction with a persistantly patriarchal social and cultural order.

Second, the world-wide pressures of liberal feminists and advocates of women's rights towards eliminating gender-based discrimination, using the United Nations for promoting women's rights. The United Nations Decade for Women (1975–85) and specific UN meetings (Mexico City, 1975; Copenhagen, 1980; Nairobi, 1985; Beijing, 1995) required governments to send official delegations and, at least rhetorically, to address the issues of women's rights. Debates over women's rights and gender-based discrimination were injected into official politics in the Middle East, as they were everywhere else. The formation of official women's organizations in various

countries, including Middle Eastern societies from the 1960s onward, and the rise of 'state-sponsored feminism' must be seen in
this light. Feminism, as an official policy for promoting women's
rights in the family and the workplace, was imposed on governments where, for lack of democratic freedoms and civil liberties, a
viable civil society was non-existent. Nevertheless, this doctrinal
innovation was bound to affect gender awareness and the lives of
men and women, encouraging a vital women's movement for equality; with this ideological influence came the global currency of such
feminist concepts as patriarchy and women's subordination. The
movement could be circumscribed, its messages expropriated, misrepresented, distorted and subjected to hostile mockery and to
political attacks. Feminism could be pushed into individualism, into
self-indulgence and complacency, become increasingly oblivious to
the concerns of the least privileged and the most oppressed; feminists could be compromised by becoming part of officialdom or
being co-opted by patriarchal states. But feminist ideas and messages
and feminist analysis of male power in its diversity and the justice
of feminist demands could not be extinguished.

Thus, with the rise of the new fundamentalist movements in the
Middle East following the 1979 Revolution in Iran, women, more
than any other group, posed the most urgent challenge, in words
and in actions, to re-Islamification policies. This happened in all
countries where fundamentalists captured state power: in Pakistan
under Zia ul-Haq, in present-day Sudan, and in Iran as well as in
Algeria, where women are caught between the FIS and the Algerian
state terrorism. Even in Afghanistan, where the impact of war and
the civilian population's day-to-day concern for mere survival are
nightmarish preoccupations of the international relief community,
women and women's rights have been a major, if not the major
reason for the world's condemnation of policies of the Afghani
Mujahedin and their Taliban successor.

Within this context, and much to the dismay of the fundamentalists, women emerged as a political force in the Middle East,
baffling regimes and their opponents alike. Feminism and feminist
demands and their compatibility with Islam have been imposed on
the agenda of Islamic states and movements throughout the region,

and, through them, on the agenda of secular nationalists, socia,
and international feminists as never before. As was mentioned in
Chapter 6, in this, the experiences of Iranian women under Islamic
rule have been crucial.

Debates over Islam and women's rights, and 'Islamic feminism',
were revived in Iran immediately after the Revolution, with the
Islamification of women's rights in family and workplace and with
the cultural import of conservative Qur'anic interpretations — but
also with women's remarkable resistance in reclaiming their rights
and the retreats they have imposed on the government. Within Iran,
the Islamists' policies and practices aim to counter feminist ideas
and to silence activists who struggle for gender democracy, going
beyond the acceptable Islamic legal and political boundaries. The
repressive intent is transparent. But to others in the Middle East and
North Africa, Iran seems to offer the hope for a society based on
the Islamic moral and ethical principles of the seventh-century
Arabian Peninsula. Iran introduced the first Islamic fundamentalist
state, coming to power through a mass-based revolutionary movement. Besides, with ravaging civil war, and internal political and
military conflicts in Afghanistan and Sudan, Iran has become, by
default, the crucial model of a 'successful' Islamic polity. At the
gates of the twenty-first century, Iran presents a new revolutionary
project to intellectuals frustrated by a bleak modernity, an 'authentic',
'indigenous' substitute for the capitalist model of growth and its
uninviting social and moral consequences.

The Islamists' manipulative use of gender issues and feminist
concepts has led to confusion for many secular intellectuals, including
feminists, who have placed debate over 'Islamic feminism' on the
agenda, some embracing it with enthusiasm, others rejecting it with
passion. As it happens, the debate by secular Iranian feminists over
these issues is more passionate and persistent than among other
feminists of Middle Eastern background. But the relevance of this
question extends beyond Iran. This debate situates ideological struggle
on ground where the basic frame of reference has been determined
by the fundamentalists; a terrain which is at odds with the needs,
interests and the familiar vocabulary of secular feminist academics,
researchers and activists both within and outside Islamic societies.

## 'Muslim' Feminism and Gender Activism

The positions taken by secular feminists and scholars on the concept of Islamic feminism are various. One group, some with roots in the organized left, adamantly rejects the possibility of co-existence between Islam and feminism. They are not impressed by Islam's internal variations or the impact of local economic, cultural and ethnic factors in nuancing the effects of traditional practices on women's subordination. For them, hostility towards feminism and feminist demands is inherent in divine laws, and women's liberation in Islamic societies must therefore start with de-Islamization of every aspect of life. Hence, feminism and Islam cannot be reconciled (Azad, 1997: 158–9; Khayam, 1998: 12; Shafiq, 1998: 14). At the other extreme are those who posit that feminism within an Islamic framework is the only culturally sound and effective strategy for the region's women's movement. They see Islamic feminism as 'a feminism true to its society's traditions', and 'a resistance to cultural conversion', endeavouring 'to release western women's claim on feminism' (El Guindi, 1996: 159–61; Majid, 1998).

In a certain sense, the notion of 'Islamic feminism' may be an oxymoron (Mojab, 1995: 25; Shahidian, 1997: 51). The term, nevertheless, is used increasingly to identify the beliefs and activities of Muslim women who are trying to improve the lot of their sex within the confines of their faith. As a matter of political expediency, secular women, as well, have made use of an Islamic framework in demanding change. An increasing number of secular Middle Eastern feminist scholars have turned to Islamic texts to find solutions for women's oppression. The reasons are various. As Hisham Sharabi notes, '[i]nvoking Islam' has become a 'measure of self-defense' among such scholars, and 'a ritualistic act for even the most outspoken among them' (Sharabi, 1992: 131). It may also be that the political and discursive influence of Islamic fundamentalism is so sublimely apparent and seems so unbudgeable that a large section of Middle Eastern academics and intellectuals are taking it for granted as inevitable. It seems that we live in an era in Middle Eastern history in which Islamic fundamentalism cannot be challenged. Secular discourse to promote gender equality has been discredited as 'elitist', modernist or 'white' and 'North-oriented', and leftists and nationalists are told, in effect, that we must revisit our beliefs, our theories and our politics – that we must first affirm Islam, even its treatment of women, before we dare to speak of women's oppression in Islamic societies. To secure credibility one should choose Islam over modernity, pretend that one has done so and always use Islam as an analytical category, a political ideology and a cultural identity before even starting to discuss women's status in Islamic societies.

This is a difficult personal intellectual and political choice for secular scholars. The choice must be respected. But it may also be a choice which reflects the drift of professional opportunity or what Terry Eagleton has called 'taking on the colour of historical environs' (Eagleton, 1996: 23). It can also express a terrible exhaustion, a sense of defeat. In any case, theorization of Islam's promise, which relies on twisting facts or distorting realities, ignoring or hiding that which should be clear, is no service to feminism or to the women of the region. Obscuring what should be plain takes away the choices of others. Worse, it may justify the actions of those who take away the choice.

These problems arise when women in Islamic societies are reduced to their 'Islamic' identity or when political Islam is presented as the only terrain on which legitimate or effective discourse can be developed, or when Islamic feminism is proposed as the only banner under which the region's women should fight for justice and equality. In this case, clearly, we are not talking about a healthy political heterogeneity, plurality and diversity, or about different strategies which feminists can honestly adopt to pursue women's interests. The problem arises, instead, when enthusiasts insist that Islam is all there is in the Middle East. Then 'Islamic' identity becomes the 'one size fits all' robe that all women (and men) are forced to wear.

It is perfectly proper, for example, to suggest, as Abdullahi An-Na'im does, that the advocates of women's human rights in Islamic societies should educate themselves in the concepts and techniques of Islamic discourse (An-Na'im, 1995: 59). As Nawal El Saadawi argues, rereading one's history and understanding one's culture is essential for nationalist, socialist and feminist movements in order to 'build themselves on a firm base, to discover their roots' (El Saadawi, 1997: 246). This historical identification is needed for any progressive movement in order to maintain its perspective, specificity and originality. However, it is quite wrong in my view to advise advocates of women's rights, as Anouar Majid does, that Islam and the Islamic view is the only culturally legitimate frame of reference within which to campaign for women's rights (Majid, 1998: 322). For Majid, Islamic feminism, rhapsodically, is the 'revolutionary paradigm' of our time, its scope so large and so 'thoroughly revolutionary' that 'it may well be one of the best platforms from which to resist the effects of global capitalism' and thus to contribute to a 'rich, egalitarian, polycentric world' (Majid, 1998: 355).

Along the same lines, it is unsound advice that women should try to 'diminish, rather than emphasize the significance of differences between religious and secular discourses' in order to 'rehabilitate secularism, itself, from its present negative, anti-religious and colonial associations among the masses of Muslims' (An-Na'im, 1995: 52, 54). While An-Na'im, unlike Majid, emphasizes that 'the need for human rights advocates to engage in an Islamic discourse does not mean that it should be the only type of frame of reference they should adopt' (An-Na'im, 1995: 59), the reader is still left with the impression that the Islamic solution, in the end, is the final solution. For Majid, Islam is the best solution,especially when decorated with 'democratic' phrases; for An-Na'im, it may not be the best, but, fatalistically, under present circumstances, it is the only solution that is likely to be understood.

The same kind of defensiveness and defeatism can be found in Afary's argument. She does not propose an Islamic strategy, but argues that 'to avoid the charge by fundamentalists and others that feminism is a tool of imperialist governments, a feminist education should begin with a comparative view that focuses on the subordinate role of women in major religions (not just Islam)' (Afary, 1997: 110). Thus it is only after 'a discussion of the chastity belts that the European Crusaders forced on their wives ... through the job discrimination, sexual violence, and the abusive relationships that so many women in the West face today' that one may discuss the 'lives of women who live under Muslim laws'. No doubt, a comparative view helps when beginning discussion about women in Islamic societies. But why must women's rights advocates delay criticism of Islam until they complete the ritual of bashing the West? Why not also, for example, discuss how and what women in the West succeeded in gaining in terms of legal equality once the sanctity of the state's shell was finally torn off, removing the possibility of invoking holy laws to deny women their human rights? Why not discuss what is achievable and has been actually achieved by women in the West as a result of their struggle to remove discriminatory barriers in public life?

I would present two arguments here. First, I would suggest that it is exactly the populist concern for 'rehabilitating' oneself in the 'eyes of the masses' which has throttled radical intellectuals and caused initiatives to halt the march of fundamentalism to dry out. What has been accomplished? The masses have been persuaded by the fundamentalists that a return to religion is the only answer to their problems – and that there are even some rewards to be gained if they will express their grievances through formulas invoking 'Islamic identity'. To avoid alienating the masses, the intellectuals have kept quiet, sacrificing what they had won over many decades in the struggle for democracy and national liberation. Should intellectuals continue to blur their own views – apologize for their secularism, even turn to religion – because religion has been presented to the masses as the only genuine, home-grown vehicle for national liberation, and thus avoid asserting their own identities? Has not this populist yearning to sound like, look like and be like the masses, the desire 'to have one voice against imperialism' (Khomeini's magic motto, *vahdat-e kalameh*, unity of words), enormously assisted dictatorial rulers and leaders in the region? For the dictators too, for their own purposes, claim that they speak for, act for and decide for the whole society and insist that they represent the interests of all.

Second, the best way to support the struggles of women in the Middle East is not to erase differences among them or to play down the basic distinction between secular and Islamist visions. To privilege the voice of religion and celebrate 'Islamic feminism' is to highlight only one of the many forms of identity available to Middle Eastern women, obscuring ways that identity is asserted or reclaimed, overshadowing forms of struggle outside religious practices and silencing the secular voices which are still raised against the region's stifling Islamification policies.

In this context, I find problematic the attempts of some feminist academics of Middle Eastern background who have started to identify themselves as 'Muslim women' – even though they have absolutely nothing in common with the Muslim lifestyle that they defend, and may have spent hardly any part of their adult lives in their native countries. While scholars like Fatima Mernissi are careful with the term, others use it loosely, implicitly proposing that all women who live in Islamic societies are not merely subjects of a Muslim state but active believers. For Mernissi, being a 'Muslim' means being subject to the control of a theocratic state, stressing that

> What the individual thinks is secondary for this definition. Being Marxist or Maoist or atheist does not keep one from obeying the national laws, those of the theocratic state, which define the crimes and set the punishments. Being Muslim is a civil matter, a national identity, a passport, a family code of laws, a code of public rights. (Mernissi, 1991: 20–1)

Mernissi cautions intellectuals not to confuse Islam as belief and personal choice, and Islam as law, as state religion. This is sound advice. But we are frequently confronted with usages which blur the distinction. As a matter of individual choice, it is, of course, perfectly fine to blend a modern lifestyle which supports individual development and personal freedom with an equally strong sense of belonging to a community, wishing in this way to recover one's culture and history. One can have no objection, for example, to a feminist academic scholar of Middle Eastern background who, for whatever reason, feels the need to identify herself as a Muslim woman. Shahla Haeri, for example, explains the double dilemma she faces when talking about Muslim women in the United States (her writing deals with Muslim women in Iran and Pakistan). In contrast to the image of Muslim women dominant in the West (which is always one of veiled, secluded, ever-passive, victimized, mute, immobile and obedient creatures), Haeri announces, 'I am a Muslim woman ... and I do not see myself and my Muslim friends in the exotic and occidental "imagining" of Muslim women' (Haeri, 1995: 132). She then describes the 'Muslim women' that she identifies with and writes about. These are proud women 'threatening to the "establishment Islam" and to the fundamentalists'. They are 'unveiled, autonomous, independent, economically successful, educated, and articulate women'.

Haeri's adoption of 'Muslim' identity draws attention to the diverse and differentiated groups of women categorized or self-identified as 'Muslim women' in the West. Her apparent intention is to bring to the fore Muslim women's agency and empowerment – not despite the veil and segregation, but because of them. There is also no question that there are autonomous 'Muslim women' like Haeri in the West, and that some also live, however precariously, in Islamic societies. But Haeri focuses on a small minority. Can this category be transposed to another context, to the majority of women living in the regimented Islamic states of Iran or Pakistan under religious laws? Their situation is different. Caught in conflicting roles, brutalized by legal and extra-legal oppressive practices and traditions, the vast majority are not the 'unveiled, autonomous and educated' women given to us by Haeri. These majority women, subjects of a strict and ever-watchful Islamic state, do not have Haeri's choices open to them.

Privileged by modern legal and democratic institutions in adopted countries which, apparently, give them the choice to put on or take off their Muslim identity as they wish, scholars like Haeri exoticize difference, turning a grim political reality at home into what seems a merely playful intellectual exercise. They overlook the critical importance of the element of choice (which they have) and the existence of legal and democratic institutions which protect it in the West – forgetting that these choices and democratic rights are painfully missing for women who live under Islamic rule. Indeed, this habit brings to mind the Persian proverb about 'the pleasant sound of the distant drum' (*aavaz-e dohol shenidan az dour khoush a'st*) – a popular saying used by Persian poets and philosophers critical of the illusions created in the name of distant, remote and improbable things.

## Silencing the Secular Voices

Let us look again at the properties of 'feminist' and 'Islamic' in their broadest sense. As two distinct signifiers, each of these words denotes

certain observable features in the discourse and vision of an individual or political movement. Elsewhere I have proposed that being
a 'feminist' begins with the refusal to subordinate one's life to the
male-centred dictates of religious and non-religious institutions.
Feminism's core idea is that women and men are biologically
different, but this difference should not be translated into an unequal valuation of women's and men's experience; biology should
not lead to differences in legal status, the privileging of one over
the other.

This idea is diametrically opposed to the basic principles of Islam.
As I have already discussed in Chapter 1, the Qur'an makes men 'the
managers (Qawwamoun) of the affairs of women', because 'God has
made the one to excel over the other,' assigning men the task of
admonishing women when they fear they may be rebellious.[4] In
fact, women are a 'tillage' for the male believer. He can come unto
his 'tilth as he wishes and forward his soul'.[5] Of course, there are
significant differences among various interpretations of the Qur'an
and the Islamic laws and instructions. The fact has already been
stressed that Islam, like other religions and ideologies, has a contingent character; it has a remarkable capacity to adapt to different
indigenous cultures and societies and economic and political conditions. This means that there are many different ways that Islam
can be adopted. But no amount of twisting and bending can reconcile the Qur'anic injunctions and instructions about women's
rights and obligations with the idea of gender equality. Regardless
of the interpretation of the Qur'an and the Shari'a, if the Qur'anic
instructions are taken literally, Islamic individuals or societies cannot favour equal rights for women in the family or in certain areas
of social life. As Maxime Rodinson has observed, 'whereas Muslims
may have different interpretations of the social, economic, or political implications of Islam, their perception of the moral features of
their religion is almost unchanging' (Rodinson cited in Ayubi, 1995:
89). We are repeatedly reminded by the Islamists and their supporters that the Qur'an makes men and women equal in the eyes of
God.[6] But this does not mean that their rights and obligations on
earth are or should be the same. We should also be aware that the
rules laid down in the Qur'an and the hadith are directly incorpo-

rated into the civil and criminal codes that regulate gender relations in almost all Islamic societies. I demonstrated the impact of this Islamic legislation in my discussion of women's life under fundamentalist rule in Iran.

What conclusion can be drawn from these arguments? Is it that Islam and feminism are not compatible? The answer is tangled. Certainly, there are women who demand equal rights and who have yet adopted Islam as their personal faith, as a cultural identity and as a response to spiritual needs in a world increasingly engulfed in spiritual impoverishment. Which is to say, such a person might call herself a 'Muslim' feminist, aspiring to feminist goals. In such a case, she has left behind the Islamic legal framework on matters of women's rights and status, even though she may not know it or may not wish to acknowledge it. If, however, this same person considers herself a feminist (or is so identified by others) and claims at the same time that the Shari'a is the legitimate framework for achieving feminist goals, then we are compelled to redefine both feminism and the Shari'a, since Shari'a distinguishes between the rights of human beings on the basis of sex (and religion). The Shari'a unapologetically discriminates against women and religious minorities. If the principles of the Shari'a are to be maintained, women cannot be treated any better. Women cannot enjoy equality before the law and in law. The Shari'a is not compatible with the principles of equality of human beings.

This introduces a new problem. For, as Terry Eagleton argues, 'any term which tries to cover everything would end up meaning nothing in particular, since signs work by virtue of their differences' (Eagleton, 1996: 103). If terms such as 'feminist' and 'Islamic' are to mean anything, there must be something with which they are different, that is, the Shari'a-based idea of equality. This includes only those who, under the Shari'a, must be treated equally. As Elizabeth Mayer notes, this is why some Muslims argue that 'Islam recognizes the principle of equality', while at the same time 'they maintain that women and non-Muslims must be accorded an inferior status' (Mayer, 1995: 80). Thus, if one is a believer in the fundamentals of the faith and accepts the Qur'an as the word of God – as Muslims do – then, for her, the Qur'anic laws and instructions on such an important question as equality are beyond human intervention. In that case, she inevitably has to accept the justice of sexual hierarchy within the family and in society, as stipulated in the Qur'an and regulated through Islamic laws. This person may call herself a feminist, but she cannot believe in both the Islamic and feminist concepts of equality. The two notions of equality are not compatible.

Which is to say, Islam is reconcilable with feminism only when Islamic or Muslim identity is reduced to a matter of mere spiritual and cultural affiliation, because any meaningful change in the treatment of women in Islamic societies has to start by the recognition of women as autonomous full citizens, which includes legal equality for women in family law and other civil legislation. If we agree that, as Chantal Mouffe notes, feminist politics is 'the pursuit of feminist goals and aims' which should consist 'in the transformation of all the discourses, practices and social relations where the category "woman" is constructed in a way that implies subrdination' (Mouffe, 1995: 329), then Islamic feminism as an alternative to Europe-based feminism will not take us on the road to transform all relations and structures of subordination. That is to say, change in Islamic societies is multi-dimensional. But it has to start, perhaps, with the rule of law, state accountability and separation of state from religion. This makes feminism as a practical project virtually inconceivable within the legal, political and moral framework of Islamic fundamentalism. For in a fundamentalist regime, affiliative signals are never enough; the essentials of belief are laid down as prescriptions, and they have to be obeyed. There is an intrusion of state power. This important element, more often than not, gets lost in the discourses of 'Islamic' feminists.

Not surprisingly, this is a contested issue. The scholars who harbour heady enthusiasm for Islamic feminism very often neglect the crucial distinction between Islam as a legal and political system and Islam as spiritual and moral guidance. As an example of such a position we can use an intervention by Afsaneh Najmabadi, a respected proponent of Islamic feminism. Soberly enough, Najmabadi starts with a strategic recognition of the ideological monopoly exercised by the Iranian clerics, noting, as one result, that on women's issues, feminism and Islamic thought are represented as two distinct and self-contained, contradictory viewpoints. But this polarity, she feels, is overdrawn. Calling our attention to the new energy expressed by Iranian women, Najmabadi claims that this enlarged presence, in her words, so 'vivacious' and 'exhilarant', should *not* be seen as an angry response to the woman-negating policies of the Islamic Republic, but, on the contrary, should be viewed as a *positive* result of the Islamists' ascent to power. For the exhilarated and exhilarating new voices are those of women who, prior to the Revolution, had been driven to the margins of Iranian culture and politics – Muslim women, who are now finding their way towards an authentic Islamic feminism (Najmabadi, 1995).

Indeed, with the new regime's transformation of ideas about women and femininity, these previously excluded, religious women, 'in concurrence with these [fundamentalists' ideas]' have managed to make social life more 'woman-inclusive' (*zan-shomoul*). To underscore this argument, Najmabadi points to the journal *Zanan* as a forum which has 'opened an important historical moment for dialogue between Muslim and non-Muslim, secular and religious feminists', and then – through a lengthy rereading and rewriting of Islamic concepts contained in *Zanan* articles – concludes that discrimination by sex is *not* of Islamic origin, but is the result, instead, of 'historically rooted' (and, therefore, one supposes, reversible) 'misconceptions'. Urging upon her readers the reconstruction of such categories as independence, freedom and women's right to choose, but always '*within the Islamic frame*' (my emphasis), Najmabadi assures us that such concepts can be made 'central' to feminist writings on women and femininity, establishing 'fertile ground' for sisterly 'dialogue, cooperation and solidarity' (Najmabadi, 1995: 182, 195). On this basis (that is, on the basis of a virtual capitulation by secular feminists to the demands of the religious text), the antinomies of 'feminism' and 'Islam' can be reconciled.

I would argue that this is a reconciliation in words only, a reconciliation accomplished through the manipulation of belief. As a matter of principle, the Islamic feminist reconstruction of clerical language touches the phrase only. It does not touch the political foundations or organizational muscle which underlie the fundamentalist project, nor can it affect substantially the economic, social and cultural crises which, these days, increasingly, force the regime to rethink its priorities. Implicit in Najmabadi's analysis is the unproven, intellectualist (or rationalist) assumption that the Islamic government will retreat on gender policy if Islamic feminists can but find the means to present a compelling argument. Clearly, it is true, as Najmabadi argues, that an attack on misogynist belief requires more than legal change. '[C]hanging the way a society thinks needs a radical revolution in culture, thought, and imagination, ... part of which [is created through] the feminist rethinking and rereading of the existing texts' (Najmabadi, 1995: 202). But, equally clearly, it is more than texts that are at stake. A 'ruthless criticism of everything existing', as Marx suggested in 1844, must be 'ruthless in two senses': fearless and unafraid of its own conclusions, and fearless and unafraid of conflict 'with the powers that be' – it must be a criticism in which the 'reform of consciousness' is achieved 'not through dogmas' (whether these dogma are stated in an old language or a new) but, as Marx reminds us, 'through analyzing the mystical [or mystified] consciousness, the consciousness which is unclear to itself, whether it appears in religious or political form' (Marx and Engels, 1978: 12–15).[7]

It must also be noted that, beyond its one-sidedness, Najmabadi's proposal seems to suggest that the rethinking and rereading must pass through the specific filter of Islamic feminism. *Zanan*, on this account, becomes a new democratic intellectual space, so that democracy (*mardom-salari*) will break its 'male-centred bonds, and become feminist and female-inclusive'. The formula, therefore, requires two steps: the reform of fundamentalist practice on gender will proceed through a reharmonization of feminist and religious thought, this understood as a 'radical revolution in culture, thought, and imagination'; and, in so doing, as a second step, the critique will necessarily start from the rhetorical premises and the space occupied by Islamic feminist theory. Thus, Najmabadi sets down what she understands as the vital intellectual centre of the debate, a 'new democratic space' repositioned within the Islamic framework. Whether secular women can make use of this 'new democratic space' (cramped as it may be) will be up to them (Najmabadi, 1995: 205).

I must emphasize that I do not argue that reading and rereading

Islamic texts from a feminist perspective is not a worthwhile project. I do not wish to make a fetish of secularism either. Disagreement among feminists over religion – whether or not Islam can be reformed – should not lead to non-negotiable conflicts which make impossible cooperation and coalitional work for improving women's rights and status in the Middle East and North Africa. But one could reasonably expect that the rereading of the *Shari'a* and other holy texts from a secular feminist perspective should aim at demonstrating the limits which the Islamic *Shari'a* provides as a chosen vehicle for changing the gender order. The problem with most rereading efforts (with a few exceptions, such as Fatima Mernissi's) is that they start with the defeatist assumption that all secular projects and discourses have failed; and that, in consequence, the discourse of gender must be an Islamic one. Implicit in these efforts is the acceptance of Islamic fundamentalist movements and regimes as the only conceivable future for societies of the Middle East where fundamentalists now rule. Hence, 'Islamic feminism' is embraced with an enthusiasm born of the most profound pessimism about the prospects for change.

Worse still, in the Islamic feminist analysis of gender politics under fundamentalist rule, no mention is made of the social, political and cultural parameters which might determine the effectiveness or failure of feminist activities in Islamic societies. Neither is attention paid to the contradictory impact of Islamic feminists' activities, that is, their role in legitimizing and sanitizing the political-religious dictatorship. The political limits which determine what one can or cannot take up as issues of women's concern are not examined. Neither is the role of political repression, or the way in which complicity is secured with state policies.

In the end, exhilarated by the 'linguistic and interpretational' experiments of their Muslim sisters, scholars like Najmabadi manage to conveniently overlook all individual, national and international evidence of cultural and political repression, say, in Iran, some of which I have discussed in Chapter 6. Entanglement in the grip of populism has meant for the advocates of Islamic feminism not the promised 'radical revolution in thought, culture and imagination', but the virtual abandonment of the secular democratic vision of feminism, sacrificing its hard-won achievements at the feet of an

'Islamic' vision of change. Instead of maintaining distinctive demands and discourse, supporting 'Islamic feminism' but, at the same
time, sharply exposing its limits and trying to elevate those demands, secular intellectuals seem to be trying to reshape and soften
their ideas to fit the ideals of an elusive 'Muslim feminism'. That is
to say, what we are witnessing is not the 'multi-lingualism' of feminism but the transformation and absorption of its secular 'language'
into a religious one, which, through discriminatory practices, is
sanitized and renamed as empowerment. Overheated excitement
about Muslim women's agency, incautiously promoting the viewpoints of the region's Muslim female elites – who, knowingly or
unknowingly, provide support for the powerful and brutal dictators
in the region – has more serious consequences. It discredits and
puts in jeopardy the non-Muslim women who, under precarious,
often frightening, conditions, are trying to reclaim women's voice
and women's space in Islamic societies.

On balance, it is clear that we need to attend directly to the
political problems involved in the ambiguous use of the concept of
'Islamic feminism'. Instead of engaging in a debate over whether or
not 'Islam' and 'feminism' are in any sense compatible, or whether
'Islamic feminism' has a realistic future before it, we need to ask,
more simply, what are the limits of this feminism? Is it playing a
constructive role in the struggle for democracy and cultural and
political pluralism in Islamic societies? Or is it an indigenized and
exotic version of Western feminism, which, despite excluding core
ideas of legal and social equity, sexual democracy and women's
control over their sexuality, is put forward by exceptionally forgiving, postmodern relativist feminists in the West? Most importantly,
what do advocates of women's rights in Islamic societies gain by
adjusting their vocabulary, their conceptual tools and their demands
to the requirements entailed by an Islamic framework? In the last
analysis, does 'Islamic feminism' draw its energy from a feminist
project for change, or is it just the fundamentalist gender politics
with feminist adornment, that is, is Islamic feminism a brand of
feminism or a brand of Islamism?

The point is that reform, particularly in developing societies, is
an extremely delicate and complicated process. The boundary

between the struggle for changing the status quo and gradually becoming part of it is slippery and narrow. To maintain the independence of one's own 'language' and not allow one's words to be transmuted into the language which is dominant, to press demands for reform to higher levels, and to make every reform, once achieved, the basis for achieving others – these are the most important aspects of a genuine reformism. In a Gramscian reading of 'the radical revolution in thought', the task of the intellectual is to eradicate illusions from the mind and imagination, disclosing specific interests which have become embedded in them and which draw sustenance from the dominant ideology. A continuous struggle must then be waged in civil society against hegemonic understandings, in an effort to create a 'counter-hegemony'. This is an enormously difficult task, especially where the legal framework protecting civil discourse is always liable to be shattered, and when, with impunity, even minor, hard-won concessions can be torn away. But 'the fact is', as Gramsci explained in 1916, 'that it is only step by step, stage by stage, that humanity has acquired an awareness of its own value and has won the right to live in independence of the schemes and the privileges of those minorities who happened to come to power at an earlier moment in history.' This awareness, Gramsci argues, develops 'through intelligent reflection ... on the reasons why certain situations exist and on the best means of transforming what have been opportunities for vassalage into triggers of rebellion and social reconstruction' (Gramsci, 1994: 20).

Finally, improvements in the quality of gender relations have only come about when women have secured the space they need to articulate oppositional discourses and countercultural politics. Such an achievement, in turn, has been conditional on the existence of a 'public sphere' – what Nancy Fraser has called a 'subaltern counter-public', which would permit women, along with other subordinated social groups, 'to formulate oppositional interpretations of their identities, interests, and needs' (Fraser, 1995: 291). By definition, a religious state prohibits such developements. It negates the most important aspect of equality, equality before the law, providing the followers of the state religion and a religiously based social order, and excluding or persecuting non-believers and non-conformists.

# Feminism and Islamic Fundamentalism

Theocratic rule is always authoritarian. And by monopolizing the 'discursive arena' for inventing, circulating and promoting (gendered) cultural, social and political values, the religious state also shrinks the chances for women to formulate 'counterdiscourses', re-encoding and subordinating any political dissent, narrowing women's options, preaching what it takes to be a singular 'truth'.

## Notes

1. Qurrat-ol 'Ayne was arrested and murdered in 1852 in Tehran, after a failed assassination attempt against the Qajar King, Naserol-Din Shah which led to the massacare of Babis in Iran (Mehrabi, 1994: 129–31).

2. Among very good studies on the early women's movment in Iran see Afary (1989, 1996); Bamdad (1977); Nahid (1360/1981); Najmabadi (1993); and Sanasarian (1982).

3. For a remarkable history of early Egyptian feminism see Shaarawi (1986). See also Badran (1994, 1995).

4. Sura IV: 35 (Women) (translated by Arberry, 1964).

5. Sura II: 223 (The Cow) (translated by Arberry, 1964).

6. Sura IV: 34 and 124 (women).

7. Marx's 'For a Ruthless Criticism of Everything Existing', printed in the form of a letter to his co-editor, Arnold Ruge, first appeared in the *Deutsche-Französische Jahrbücher* in 1844.

# References

Abu-Odeh, L. (1996) 'Crimes of Honour and the Construction of Gender in Arab Societies', in M. Yamani (ed.), *Feminism and Islam: Legal and Literary Perspectives*, New York University Press, New York.
——— (1992) 'Post-Colonial Feminism and the Veil: Thinking the Difference', *New England Law Review*, Vol. 26 (Summer).
Afary, J. (1997) 'The War Against Feminism in the Name of the Almighty: Making Sense of Gender and Muslim Fundamentalism' *New Left Review*, No. 224 (July–August).
——— (1996) 'Steering between Scylla and Charybdis: Shifting Gender Roles in Twentieth Century Iran', *National Women's Studies Association Global Perspectives*, Vol. 8, No. 1 (Spring).
——— (1989) 'On the Origins of Feminism in Early Twentieth-Century Iran', *Journal of Women's History*, Vols 1–2 (Fall).
Afkhami, M. (1994) *Women and the Law in Iran (1967–1978)* (Hoquq-e Zan Dar Iran 1967–1978), Women's Center of the Foundation for Iranian Studies, Washington DC.
——— (1984) 'Iran: A Future in the Past; "The Pre-Revolutionary" Women's Movement', in R. Morgan (ed.), *Sisterhood is Global*, Anchor Press/Doubleday, Garden City, NY.
Afshar, H. (1997) 'Women and Work in Iran', *Political Studies*, Vol. XLV, No. 4.
——— (1994) 'Women and the Politics of Fundamentalism in Iran', *Women Against Fundamentalism*, No. 5 (October).
Aghajanian, A. (1986) 'Some Notes on Divorce in Iran', *Journal of Marriage and the Family*, No. 48 (November).
Agnes, F. (1995) 'Redefining the Agenda of the Women's Movement Within a Secular Framework', in T. Sarkar and U. Butalia (eds), *Women and Right-Wing Movements: Indian Experiences*, Zed Books, London and New Jersey.
Ahmad, A. (1992) *In Theory: Classes, Nations, Literature*, Verso, London and New York.
Ahmed, A. (1992) *Postmodernism and Islam: Predicament and Promise*, Routledge, London and New York.
Ahmed, L. (1992) *Women and Gender in Islam: Historical Roots of a Modern Debate*, Yale University Press, New Haven and London.

———— (1982) 'Western Ethnocentrism and Perceptions of the Harem', *Feminist Studies*, Vol. 8, No. 8 (Fall).

Al-Azm, S.J. (1994) 'Islamic Fundamentalism Reconsidered: A Critical Outline of Problems, Ideas, and Approaches', Part 2, *South Asia Bulletin*, Vol. XIV, No. 1.

———— (1993–94) 'Islamic Fundamentalism Reconsidered: A Critical Outline of Problems, Ideas, and Approaches', Part 1, *South Asia Bulletin*, Vol. XIII, Nos 1 and 2.

———— (1981) 'Orientalism and Orientalism in Reverse', *Khamsin*, No. 8, Ithaca Press, London.

Al-Azmeh, A. (1997) 'Conversation with Aziz Al-Azmeh, "Political Islams: Modernities and Conservative-Populist Ideologies"', *Iran Bulletin*, Nos 15–16 (Spring–Summer).

———— (1993) *Islams and Modernities*, Verso, London and New York.

Al-Fanar Report (1995) 'Developments in the Struggle against the Murder of Women Against the Background of So-Called Family Honour', *Women Against Fundamentalism*, No. 6

Alloula, M. (1986) *The Colonial Harem*, University of Minnesota Press, Minneapolis.

Amin, S. and S. Hossain (1995) 'Women's Reproductive Rights and the Politics of Fundamentalism: A View from Bangladesh', *Women Against Fundamentalism*, No. 7.

Anderson, N. (1976) *Law Reform in the Muslim World*, University of London/Athlone Press, London.

An-Na'im, A. (1995) 'The Dichotomy Between Religious and Secular Discourse in Islamic Societies', in M. Afkhami (ed.), *Faith and Freedom: Women's Human Rights in the Muslim World*, Syracuse University Press, Syracuse, NY.

Arberry, J. (1964) *The Quran Interpreted*, Oxford University Press, London.

Armour, E.T. (1997) 'Crossing the Boundaries Between Deconstruction, Feminism, and Religion', in N.J. Holland (ed.), *Feminist Interpretation of Jacques Derrida*, Pennsylvania State University, Pennsylvania.

Asad, T. (1973) 'Two European Images of Non-European Rule', in T. Asad (ed.), *Anthropology and the Colonial Encounter*, Ithaca Press, New York.

————(1968) *The Idea of an Anthropology of Islam*, Occasional Papers Series, Centre for Contemporary Arab Studies, Georgetown University Press, Washington DC.

Ashrafi, G.H. (1375/1996) *Ghanoon-e Mojazat-e Eslami* (The Law of Islamic Retribution), Ganj-e Danesh Publishing House, Tehran.

Atkinson, K. (1992) 'Tales of Desire', *New Observations*, No. 88 (March–April).

Ayubi, N. (1995) 'Radical Islamism and Civil Society in the Middle East', *Contention*, Vol. 4, No. 3 (Spring).

Azad, A. (1997) 'Eslam dar barabar-e feminism' (Islam against Feminism), *Journal of Iranian Women's Studies Foundation*, No. 8 (Summer).

Azzam, M. (1996) 'Gender and the Politics of Religion in the Middle East', in M. Yamani (ed.), *Feminism and Islam: Legal and Literary Perspectives*, New York University Press, New York.

Badran. M. (1995) *Feminists, Islam and Nation*, Princeton University Press, Princeton, NJ.

———— (1994) 'Gender Activism: Feminists and Islamists in Egypt', in V.M. Moghadam (ed.), *Identity Politics and Women: Cultural Reassertions and Feminisms in*

*International Perspective*, Westview Press, Boulder, CO, San Francisco and Oxford.
────── (1993) 'Independent Women: More than a Century of Feminism in Egypt', in J. Tucker (ed.), *Arab Women: Old Boundaries, New Frontiers*, Indiana University Press, Bloomington and Indianapolis.

Bagley, F.R.C. (1971) 'The Iranian Family Protection Law of 1967: A Milestone in the Advance of Women's Rights', in C.E. Bosworth (ed.), *Islam and Iran*, Edinburgh University Press, Edinburgh.

Bamdad, B. (1977) *From Darkness into Light: Women's Emancipation in Iran*, Exposition Press, Hicksville, NY.

Bank-e Markazi-ye Iran (Central Bank of Iran) (1985) *Negahi be Tose'eh Eqtesadi pas Az Enqelab (A Glance at Economic Development After the Revolution)*, Government of Iran, Tehran.

Banoon, P. and S. Simnegar (1996) 'History of Jews in Iran: 1500–Present', in H. Sarshar and H. Adhami (eds), *Terua: The History of Contemporary Iranian Jews*, Vol. I, Center for Iranian Jewish Oral History, United States.

Baron, B. (1996) 'Tolerable Intolerance? Silence on Attacks on Women by Fundamentalists', *Contention*, Vol. 5, No. 3 (Spring).

Bennoune, K. (1995) 'S.O.S. Algeria: Women's Human Rights Under Siege', in M. Afkhami (ed.), *Faith and Freedom: Women's Human Rights in the Muslim World*, Syracuse University Press, Syracuse, NY.

Bouhdiba, A. (1985) *Sexuality in Islam*, Kegan Paul, London.

Bradley, H. (1996) 'Changing Social Structures: Class and Gender', in S. Hall, D. Held, D. Hubert and K. Thompson (eds), *Modernity: An Introduction to Modern Societies*, Blackwell, Oxford.

Bronwyne, W. (1994) 'Women, the Law, and Cultural Relativism in France: The Case of Excision', *Signs: Journal of Women in Culture and Society*, Vol. 19, No. 4.

Bullough, V.L. (1976) *Sexual Variance in Society and History*, University of Chicago Press, Chicago.

Chatterjee, P. (1992) 'Their Own Words? An Essay for Edward Said', in M. Sprinker (ed.), *Edward Said: A Critical Reader*, Blackwell, Oxford and Cambridge, MA.

Chaudhry, M.S. (1991) *Women's Rights in Islam*, Adam Publishers, Delhi.

Chaumeil, M. (1995) 'Algeria: Defend Intellectuals!', *Women Against Fundamentalism*, No. 6.

Cheriet, B. (1992) 'The Resilience of Algerian Populism', *Middle East Report*, Vol. 22, No. 1 (January–February).

Cole, J.R. (1981) 'Feminism, Class, and Islam in Turn-of-the-Century Egypt', *International Journal of Middle East Studies*, Vol. 13.

Colla, E. (1993) 'Silencing is at the Heart of My Case', *Middle East Report* Vol. 23, No. 6 (November–December).

Commins, D. (1994) 'Hasan al-Bana (1906–1949)', in A. Rahnema (ed.), *Pioneers of Islamic Revival*, Zed Books, London.

Connell, D. (1997) 'Political Islam Under Attack in Sudan', *Middle East Report*, Vol. 27, No. 1 (Winter).

Coulson, N.J. (1969) *Conflict and Tensions in Islamic Jurisprudence*, University of Chicago Press, Chicago and London.

Cummins, A. (1995) 'Taslima Nasreen and the Fight Against Fundamentalism', *Women Against Fundamentalism*, No. 6.

Davis, A. (1981) *Women, Race and Class*, Random House, New York.

Davis, D. (1984) 'Ideology, Social Class and Islamic Radicalism in Modern Egypt', in S. Amir Arjomand (ed.), *From Nationalism to Revolutionary Islam*, Macmillan, London.

De Awis, M. (1991) 'A Feminist Critique of the Gulf War', *Economic and Political Weekly*, 7 September.

Doi Abdul Rahman I. (1989) *Woman in Shariah*, Ta-Ha Publishers, London.

Donnelly, J. (1989) *Universal Human Rights in Theory and Practice*, Cornell University Press, Ithaca, NY.

Dragadze, T. (1994) ' Islam in Azerbaijan: The Position of Women', in C. Fawzi El-Solh and J. Mabro (eds), *Muslim Women's Choices: Religious Belief and Social Reality*, Berg Publishers, Oxford.

Eagleton, T. (1996) *The Illusions of Postmodernism*, Blackwell, Oxford.

Ebert, T.L. (1996) *Ludic Feminism and After: Postmodernism, Desire, and Labor in Late Capitalism*, University of Michigan Press, Ann Arbor.

Ehrenreich, B. and D. English (1979) *For Her Own Good*, Pluto, London.

Eisenstadt, S.N. (1996) 'The Jacobin Component of Fundamentalist Movements', *Contention*, Vol. 5, No. 3 (Spring).

El-Gawhary, K. (1995) 'Sex Tourism in Cairo', *Middle East Report*, Vol. 25, No. 5 (September–October).

El Guindi, F. (1996) 'Feminism Comes of Age in Islam', in S. Sabbagh (ed.), *Arab Women: Between Defiance and Restraint*, Olive Branch Press, New York.

El-Nimr, R. (1996) 'Women in Islamic Law', in M. Yamani (ed.), *Feminism and Islam: Legal and Literary Perspectives*, New York University Press, New York.

El Saadawi, N. (1997) *The Nawal El Saadawi Reader*, Zed Books, London and New York.

Enayat, H. (1973) 'The Politics of Iranology, *Iranian Studies*, Vol. VI, No. 1.

Eribon, D. (1991) *Michel Foucault*, Harvard University Press, Cambridge, MA.

Ettehadieh, M. (1982) *Khaterat-e Taj-ol-Saltaneh* (Taj-ol-Saltaneh: Memoirs), Nashr-e Ketab, Tehran.

Fakhro, M. (1996) 'Gulf Women and Islamic Law', in M.Yamani (ed.), *Feminism and Islam: Legal and Literary Perspectives*, New York University Press, New York.

Farsoun, S.K. and L. Hajjar (1990) 'The Contemporary Sociology of the Middle East: An Assessment', in H. Sharabi (ed.), *Theory, Politics and the Arab World: Critical Responses*, Routledge, New York and London.

Fox-Genovese, E. (1982) 'Placing Women's History in History', *New Left Review*, No. 133 (May–June).

Fraser, N. (1995) 'Politics, Culture, and the Public Sphere: Toward a Postmodern Conception', in L. Nicholson and S. Seidman (eds), *Social Postmodernism: Beyond Identity Politics*, Cambridge University Press, New York.

——— (1994) 'Michel Foucault: A "Young Conservative"?', in M. Kelly (ed.), *Critique and Power: Recasting the Foucault/Habermas Debate*, MIT Press, Cambridge, MA and London.

Gallagher, N. (1995) 'Women's Human Rights on Trial in Jordan: The Triumph of Toujan al-Faisal', in M. Afkhami (ed.), *Faith and Freedom: Women's Human Rights in the Muslim World*, Syracuse University Press, Syracuse, NY.

Giroux, H. (1994) 'Living Dangerously: Identity Politics and the New Cultural Racism', in H. Giroux (ed.), *Between Borders: Pedagogy and the Politics of Cultural*

*Studies*, Routledge, New York.

Glavanis-Grantham, K. (1995) 'Women's Movement, Feminism and the National Struggle in Palestine: Unresolved Contradictions', in H. Afshar (ed.), *Women and Politics in the Third World*, Routledge, London and New York.

Graham-Brown, S. (1988) *Images of Women: The Portrayal of Women in Photography of the Middle East 1860–1950*, Quartet Books, London.

Gramsci, A. (1994) *Pre-Prison Writings*, ed. R. Bellamy, trans V. Cox, Cambridge University Press, Cambridge.

Gruenbaum, E. (1992) 'The Islamist State and Sudanese Women', *Middle East Report*, Vol. 22, No. 6 (November–December).

Habermas, J. (1993) 'Modernity – An Incomplete Project', in T. Docherty (ed.), *Postmodernism: A Reader*, Columbia University Press, New York.

Haddad, Y. (1994) 'Muhammad Abduh: Pioneer of Islamic Reform', in A. Rahnema (ed.), *Pioneers of Islamic Revival*, Zed Books, London.

Haddad, Y.Y. and J.I. Smith (1996) 'Women in Islam: "The Mother of All Battles"', in S. Sabbagh (ed.), *Arab Women: Between Defiance and Restraint*, Olive Branch Press, New York.

Haeri, S. (1995) 'On Feminism and Fundamentalism in Iran and Pakistan', *Contention*, Vol. 4, No. 3 (Spring).

———— (1989) *Law of Desire: Temporary Marriage in Shi'i Iran*, Syracuse University Press, Syracuse, NY.

Hale, S. (1997) 'On Nuba Women and Children', *Middle East Report*, Vol. 27, No. 4 (October–December).

———— (1996) *Gender Politics in Sudan: Islamism, Socialism, and the State*, Westview Press, Boulder, CO.

Hall, S. (1996) 'The Question of Cultural Identity', in S. Hall, D. Held, Dan Hubert and K. Thompson (eds), *Modernity: An Introduction to Modern Societies*, Blackwell, Oxford.

Hamilton, R. (1980) *The Liberation of Women: A Study of Patriarchy and Capitalism*, George Allen & Unwin, London, Boston and Sydney.

Haq, F. (1996) 'Women, Islam and the State in Pakistan', *The Muslim World*, Vol. LXXXVI, No. 2 (April).

Hartman, H. (1979) 'Capitalism, Patriarchy and Job Segregation by Sex', in Z.R. Eisenstein, *Capitalist Patriarchy and the Case of Socialist Feminism*, Monthly Review Press, New York.

Harvey, D. (1990) *The Condition of Postmodernity: An Enquiry into the Origins of Cultural Change*, Blackwell, Cambridge MA and Oxford.

Hassan, R. (1992) 'Muslim Women and Post-Patriarchal Islam', in P.M. Cooey, W.R. Eakin and J.B. McDaniel (eds), *After Patriarchy: Feminist Transformations of the World Religions*, Orbis Books, Maryknoll, NY.

Hatch, E. (1983) *Culture and Morality: The Relativity of Values in Anthropology*, Columbia University Press, New York.

Hatem, M.F. (1994) 'Privatization and the Demise of "State Feminism" in Egypt', in P. Sparr (ed.), *Mortgaging Women's Lives: Feminist Critiques of Structural Adjustment*, Zed Books, London.

———— (1993) 'Toward the Development of Post-Islamist and Post-Nationalist Feminist Discourses in the Middle East', in J. Tucker (ed.), *Arab Women: Old Boundaries, New Frontiers*, Indiana University Press, Bloomington and Indianapolis.

————— (1986) 'Sexuality and Gender in Segregated Patriarchal Systems: The Case of Eighteenth- and Nineteenth-Century Egypt', Feminist Studies, Vol. 12, No. 2.

Hentsch, T. (1992) Imagining the Middle East, Black Rose Books, Montreal and New York.

Higgins (1985) 'Women in the Islamic Republic of Iran: Legal, Social, and Ideological Changes', Signs: Journal of Women in Cultures and Society, Vol. 10, No. 31.

Hill Collins, P. (1991) Black Feminist Thought: Knowledge, Consciousness, and the Politics of Empowerment. Routledge, New York and London.

Hobsbawm, E. (1994) 'Barbarism: A User's Guide', New Left Review, No. 206 (July–August).

Hoodfar, H. (1993) 'The Veil in Their Minds and On Our Heads: The Persistence of Colonial Images of Muslim Women', Resources for Feminist Research, Vol. 22, Nos 3 and 4.

Imam, A (1994) 'Politics, Islam, and Women in Kano, Northern Nigeria', in V.M. Moghadam (ed.), Identity Politics and Women: Cultural Reassertions and Feminisms in International Perspectiv, Westview Press, Boulder CO, San Francisco and Oxford.

Iran National Archives (1371/1993) Violence and Culture: Confidential Records about the Abolition of Hijab 1313–1322 H.SH, Iran National Archives, Tehran.

Iran Statistics Centre (1375/1990) Statistical Yearbook, Iran Statistics Centre, Tehran.

————— (1363/1984) Data on Large Industries, Iran Statistics Centre, Tehran.

Jaising, I. (1995) 'Violence Against Women: The Indian Perspective', in J. Peters and D. Wolper (eds), Women's Rights, Human Rights: International Feminist Perspectives, Routlege, New York and London.

Javed, N. (1993) 'Gender Identity and Muslim Women: Toll of Oppression Turned into Empowerment', Convergence, Vol. XXVII, Nos 2 and 3

Jayawardena, K. (1986) Feminism and Nationalism in the Third World, Zed Books, London and New Jersey.

Jorgensen, C. (1994) 'Women, Revolution, and Israel', in A.M. Tetreault (ed.), Women and Revolution in Africa, Asia and the New World, University of South Carolina Press.

Juergensmeyer, M. (1993) The New Cold War? Religious Nationalism Confronts the Secular State, University of California Press, Berkeley.

Kandall, T.R. (1988) The Woman Question in Classical Sociological Theory, Florida International University Press, Miami.

Kandiyoti, D. (1995) 'Reflections on the Politics of Gender in Muslim Societies: From Nairobi to Beijing', in M. Afkhami (ed.), Faith and Freedom: Women's Human Rights In The Muslim World, Syracuse University Press, Syracuse, NY.

————— (1991a) 'End of Empire: Islam, Nationalism and Women in Turkey', in D. Kandiyoti (ed.), Women, Islam and the State, Temple University Press, Philadelphia.

————— (1991b) 'Islam and Patriarchy: Comparative Perspective', in N.R. Keddie and B. Baron (eds), Women in Middle Eastern History: Shifting Boundaries in Sex and Gender, Yale University Press, New Haven and London.

Keddie, N.R. (1991) 'Introduction: Deciphering Middle Eastern Women's History', in N.R. Keddie and B. Baron (eds), Women in Middle Eastern History: Shifting Boundaries in Sex and Gender, Yale University Press, New Haven and London.

Keddie, N.R. and B. Baron (1991) (eds), Women in Middle Eastern History: Shifting

*Boundaries in Sex and Gender*, Yale University Press, New Haven and London.

Keddie, N.R. and M.E. Bonine (1981) *Modern Iran: the Dialectics of Continuity and Change*, State University of New York Press, New York.

Khayam, Z. (1998) 'Islamic Feminism: What is Your Definition?' *Arash*, No. 66 (February).

Khomeini, Ayatollah Rouhola (1366/1987) *Images of Women in the Words of Imam Khomeini* (collection of speeches), Ministry of Islamic Guidance, Tehran.

—— (1980) *Clarification of Questions*, Sadra Publisher, Qum.

Kollontai, A. (1977) *Selected Writings* (trans. A. Holt). W.W. Norton, New York.

Landau, D. (1993) *Piety and Power: The World of Jewish Fundamentalism*, Secker & Warburg, London.

Lazreg, M. (1994) *Eloquence of Silence: Algerian Women in Question*, Routledge, New York and London.

—— (1990) 'Feminism and Difference: The Perils of Writing as a Woman on Women in Algeria', in M. Horscjamd and E. Fox Keller (eds), *Conflicts in Feminism*, Routledge, London and New York.

Lovibond, S. (1989) 'Feminism and Postmodernism', *New Left Review*, No. 178 (November–December).

Lowe, L. (1991) *Critical Terrains: French and British Orientalisms*, Cornell University Press, Ithaca, NY and London.

Mabro, J. (1996) *Veiled Half-Truths: Western Travellers' Perceptions of Middle Eastern Women*, I.B. Tauris, London and New York.

McLennan, G. (1996) 'The Enlightenment Project Revisited', in S. Hall, D. Held, D. Hubert and K. Thompson (eds), *Modernity: An Introduction to Modern Societies*, Blackwell, Oxford.

Macleod, A.E. (1991) *Accommodating Protest: Working Women, the New Veiling, and Change in Cairo*, Columbia University Press, New York.

Majid, A. (1998) 'The Politics of Feminism in Islam', *Signs: Journal of Women in Culture and Society*, Vol. 23, No. 2.

Malti-Douglas, F. (1991) *Women's Body, Women's World: Gender and Discourse in Arabo-Islamic Writing*, Princeton University Press, Princeton, NJ.

Marshal, B.L. (1994) *Engendering Modernity: Feminism, Scoial Theory and Social Change*, Northeastern University Press, Boston, MA.

Marty, M. (1995) 'Comparing Fundamentalisms', *Contention*, Vol. 4, No. 2 (Winter).

Marx, K. (1984) *Preface to the Critique of Political Economy*, in *Selected Writings* (ed. D. McLellan), Oxford University Press, Oxford.

—— (1983) *Capital Vol. I*, Progress Publishers, Moscow.

—— (1973) 'The Eighteenth Brumaire of Louis Bonaparte', in *Political Writings, Vol. II: Surveys from Exile* (ed. D. Fernbach), Random House, New York.

Marx, K. and F. Engels (1978) *Marx–Engels Reader* (ed. R.C. Tucker), Norton, New York.

Marsot, A.L. (1996) 'Entrepreneurial Women in Egypt', in M. Yamani (ed.), *Feminism and Islam: Legal and Literary Perspectives*, New York University Press, New York.

Mati, L. (1990) 'Contentious Traditions: The Debate on Sati in Colonial India', in K. Sangari and V. Sudesh (eds), *Recasting Women: Essays in Indian Colonial History*, Rutgers University Press, New Brunswick, NJ.

Mayer, A.E. (1995) *Islam and Human Rights*, Westview Press, Boulder, CO.

Mehrabi, M. (1994) *Qurrat-ol-ain Shaere-e Azadikhah Va Melli Iran* (Qurrat-ol Ayne, Iran's Nationalist Libertarian Poet), Rouyesh Publications, Cologne.

Mehran, G. (1991) 'The Creation of the New Muslim Women: Female Education in the Islamic Republic of Iran', *Convergence*, International Council for Adult Education, Vol. XXIV, No. 4.

Mernissi, F. (1995) 'Arab Women's Rights and the Muslim State in the Twenty-first Century: Reflections on Islam as Religion and State', in M. Afkhami (ed.), *Faith and Freedom: Women's Human Rights in the Muslim World*, Syracuse University Press, Syracuse, NY.

——— (1992) *Islam And Democracy: Fear of the Modern World*, Addison-Wesley, Reading, MA.

——— (1991) *The Veil and the Male Elite: A Feminist Interpretation of Women's Rights in Islam*, Addison-Wesley, Reading, MA.

——— (1985) *Beyond the Veil: Male–Female Dynamics in Modern Muslim Society*, Al Saqi Books, London.

Milani, F. (1992) *Veils and Words: The Emerging Voices of Iranian Women Writers*, Syracuse University Press, Syracuse, NY.

Minai, N. (1981) *Women in Islam: Tradition and Transition in the Middle East*, Seaview Books, New York.

Ministry of Culture and Islamic Guidance (1988) *Simaay-e Zn dar Kalam-e Imam Khomeini* (Image of Women in Speeches of Imam Khomeini), Ministry of Culture and Islamic Guidance, Tehran.

Mir-Hoseinin, Z. (1996) 'Stretching the Limits: A Feminist Reading of The Sharia in Post-Khomeini Iran', in M. Yamani (ed.), *Feminism and Islam: Legal and Literary Perspectives*, New York University Press, New York.

Mitchell, R. (1987) 'The Islamic Movement: The Current Condition and Future Prospects', in B. Freyer (ed.), *The Islamic Impulse*, George Washington University, Washington, DC.

Moghadam, V. (1995) 'Women's Employment Issues in Contemporary Iran: Problems and Prospects in the 1990s', *Iranian Studies*, Vol. 28, Nos 3 and 4 (Summer–Fall).

——— (1991) 'Islamist Movements and Women's Response in the Middle East', *Gender and History*, Vol. 3, No. 3 (Autumn).

——— (1988) 'Women, Work and Ideology in the Islamic Republic of Iran', *International Journal of Middle East Studies*, Vol. 20.

Moghissi, H. (1995) 'Public Life and Women's Resistance', in S. Rahnema and S. Behdad (eds), *Iran After The Revolution: Crisis of an Islamic State*, I.B. Tauris, London and New York.

——— (1994) *Populism and Feminism in Iran: Women's Struggle in a Male-Defined Revolutionary Movement*, Macmillan Press, London.

Mojab, S. (1995). 'Islamic Feminism: Alternative or Contradiction?', *Fireweed*, No. 47 (Winter).

Moore, B. Jr (1967) *Social Origins of Dictatorship and Democracy: Lord and Peasant in the Making of the Modern World*, Beacon Press, Boston, MA.

Motahhari, M. (1358/1979) *Nezm-e Huquq-e Zan Dar Islam* (The System of Women's Rights in Islam), Sadra Publishers, Qum.

Mouffe, C. (1995) 'Feminism, Citizenship, and Radical Democratic Politics', in L. Nicholson and S. Seidman (eds), *Social Postmodernism: Beyond Identity Politics*,

Cambridge University Press, Cambridge.

Mumtaz, K and F. Shaheed (1987) *Women of Pakistan: Two Steps Forward, One Step Back?*, Zed Books, London and New Jersey.

Munson, H., JR (1996) 'Intolerable Tolerance: Western Academia and Islamic Fundamentalism', *Contention*, Vol. 5, No. 3 (Spring).

Nahid, Abd-ul-Husain (1981) *Zanan-e Iran dar Junbesh-e Mashruta* (Iranian Women: The Constitutional Revolution), n.p, Tehran.

Najmabadi, A. (1995) 'Salhay-e Osrat, Salhay-e Rouyesh' (Years of Misery, Years of Growth), *Kankash*, No. 12 (Fall), New York.

———— (1993) 'Zanha-yi Millat: Women or Wives of the Nation?', *Iranian Studies*, Vol. 26, Nos 1 and 2 (Winter/Spring).

Nasr, K.B. (1997) *Arab and Israeli Terrorism*, McFarland, Jefferson, NC.

Nateq, H. (1990) *Iran Dar Rahyabiy-e Farhangi 1834–1848* (La Perse traillée entre deux cultures), Khavaran, Paris.

———— (1984) 'Saraghaz-e Ghodrat-e Siasi va Eghtesadiy-e Molayan' (The Beginning of Clerical Economic and Political Power), *Alefba*, Second period, Vol. 2, Paris.

———— (1358/1980) 'Negahi b-e Barkhi Neveshte-ha va Mobarezat-e Zanan dar Doran Mashrutiat' (A Glance at Some of the Writings and Struggles of Women During the Constitutional Revolution), *Ketab-e Jom'eh*, No. 30.

Nederveen Pieterse, J. and B. Parekh (eds) (1995) *The Colonization of Imagination: Culture, Knowledge and Power*, Zed Books, London and New Jersey.

Nicholson, L. and S. Seidman (eds), (1995) *Social Postmodernism: Beyond Identity Politics*, Cambridge University Press, Cambridge.

Norton, A. (1991) 'Gender, Sexuality and the Iraq of Our Imagination', *Middle East Report*, Vol. 21, No. 4 (July–August).

Osborne, M.L. (1979) *Women in Western Thought*, Random House, New York.

Ostadmalek, F. (1367/1988) *Hijab va Kashf-e Hijab Dar Iran* (The Veil and Unveiling in Iran), Ataii Publishing House, Tehran.

Paidar, P. (1996) 'Feminism and Islam in Iran', in D. Kandiyoti (ed.), *Gendering the Middle East: Emerging Perspectives*, Syracuse University Press, Syracuse, NY.

Patel, V. (1994) 'Impressions of Asian Life in Britain', *Women Against Fundamentalism*. No. 5.

Rahnema, A. (1994) (ed.), *Pioneers of Islamic Revival*, Zed Books, London and New Jersey.

Rahnema, A. and F. Nomani (1990) *The Secular Miracle*, Zed Books, London and New Jersey.

Rahnema, S. (1990) 'Multinationals and Iranian Industry: 1957–1979', *Journal of Developing Areas*, Vol. 24, No. 3.

Ramazani (1993) 'Women in Iran: The Revolutionary Ebb and Flow', *Middle East Journal*, Vol. 47, No. 3 (Summer).

Rastegar, A. (1996) 'Health Policy and Medical Education', in S. Rahnema and S. Behdad (eds), *Iran After the Revolution: Crisis of an Islamic State*, I.B. Tauris, London and New York.

Rattansi, A. (1994) '"Western" Racism, Ethnicities and Identities in a "Postmodern" Frame', in A. Rattansi and S. Westwood (eds), *Racism, Modernity and Identity on the Western Front*, Polity Press, Cambridge.

Rattansi, A. and S. Westwood (1994) 'Modern Racism, Racialized Identities', in

A. Rattansi and S. Westwood (eds), *Racism, Modernity and Identity on the Western Front*, Polity Press, Cambridge.

Ritzer, G. (1992) *The McDonaldization of Society*, Sage, London.

Robbins, B. (1992) 'The East is a Career: Edward Said and the Logics of Professionalism', in M. Sprinker (ed.), *Edward Said: A Critical Reader*, Blackwell, Oxford and Cambridge, MA.

Rodinson, M. (1973) *Islam and Capitalism*, Pantheon Books, New York.

Rosen, S. (1995) *The Mask of Enlightenment: Nietzche's Zarathustra*, Cambridge University Press, Cambridge.

Roy, O. (1997) 'Rivalries and Power Plays in Afghanistan: The Taliban, the Shari'a and the Pipeline', *Middle East Report*, Vol. 27, No. 1 (Winter).

Sabbagh, S. (1996), 'Introduction: The Debate on Arab Women', in S. Sabbagh (ed.), *Arab Women: Between Defiance and Restraint*, Olive Branch Press, New York.

Sabbah, F. (1988) *Women in the Muslim Unconscious*, Pergamon Press, Oxford.

Sahgal, G. and N. Yuval-Davis (eds) (1992) *Refusing Holy Orders: Women and Fundamentalism in Britain*, Virago Press, London.

Said, E.W. (1985) 'Orientalism Reconsidered', in *Arab Society: Continuity and Change*, Croom Helm, London.

———— (1978) *Orientalism: Western Conceptions of the Orient*, Penguin, London.

Sanasarian, E. (1983) *The Women's Rights Movement in Iran: Mutiny, Appeasement, and Repression from 1900 to Khomeini*, Praeger Publishers, London.

Sarshar, H. (1996) *The History of Contemporary Iranian Jews*, Center for Iranian Jewish Oral History, Beverly Hills, CA.

Sayers, J. (1986) 'For Engels: Psychoanalytic Perspectives', in J. Sayers, M. Evans and N. Redclift (eds), *Engels Revisited: New Feminist Essays*, Tavistock Publications, London and New York.

Sayigh, R. (1981) 'Roles and Functions of Arab Women', *Arab Studies Quarterly*, Vol. 3, No. 3.

Shaarawi, H. (1986), *Harem Years: The Memoirs of an Egyptian Feminist* (trans. and introduced by M. Badran), Virago, London.

Shafiq, S. (1998) 'Islamic Feminism: What is Your Definition?', *Arash*, No. 66 (February), Paris.

Shahidian, H. (1997) 'The Politics of the Veil: Reflections on Symbolism, Islam and Feminism', *Thamyris*, Vol. 4, No. 2 (Autumn).

Sharabi, H. (1992) 'Modernity and Islamic Revival: The Critical Task of Arab Intellectuals', *Contention*, Vol. 2, No. 1 (Fall).

Sharoni, S. (1997) 'Women and Gender in Middle East Studies: Trends, Prospects and Challenges', *Middle East Report*, Vol. 27, No. 205 (October–December).

Shepard, W. (1987) 'Islam and Ideology: Towards a Typology', *International Journal of Middle East Studies*, Vol. 19.

Shukrallah, H. (1994) 'The Impact of the Islamic Movement in Egypt', *Feminist Review*, No. 47 (Summer).

Siddiqui, M. (1996) 'Law and the Desire for Social Contract: An Insight into the Hanafi Concept of Kafa'a with Reference to the Fatwa 'Alamgiri (1664–1672)', in M. Yamani (ed.), *Feminism and Islam: Legal and Literary Perspectives*, New York University Press, New York.

Smith, N. (1984) *Rabia' the Mystic and Her Fellow-Saints in Islam*, Cambridge University Press, Cambridge.

Stannard, D. (1992) *The American Holocaust: The Conquest of the New World*, Oxford University Press, Oxford and New York.

Stansell, C. (1992) 'White Feminists and Black Realities: The Politics of Authenticity', in T. Morrison (ed.), *Rac-ing Justice, En-gendering Power: Essays on Anita Hill, Clarence Thomas, and the Construction of Social Reality*, Pantheon Books, New York.

Tabari, A. and N. Yaganeh (1982) *In the Shadow of Islam: The Women's Movement in Iran*, Zed Books, London.

Tannahill, R. (1989) *Sex in History*, Sphere, London.

Taraki, L. (1996) 'Jordanian Islamists and the Agenda for Women: Between Discourse and Practice', *Middle Eastern Studies*, Vol. 32, No. 1 (January).

Tessler, M. and J. Jesse (1996) 'Gender and Support for Islamist Movements: Evidence from Egypt, Kuwait and Palestine', *The Muslim World*, Vol. LXXXVI, No. 2.

Tibi, B. (1988) *The Crisis of Modern Islam: A Preindustrial Culture in the Scientific-Technological Age*, University of Utah Press, Salt Lake City.

Tijssen, L.V.V. (1991) 'Women Between Modernity and Postmodernity', in B.S. Turner (ed.), *Theories of Modernity and Postmodernity*, Sage Publications, London.

Tohidi, N. (1994) 'Modernity, Islamization, and Women in Iran', in V. Moghadam (ed.), *Gender and National Identity: Women and Politics in Muslim Societies*, Zed Books, London.

Tucker, J. (1990) 'Taming the West: Trends in the Writing of Modern Arab Social History in Anglophone Academia', in H. Sharabi (ed.), *Theory, Politics and the Arab World: Critical Responses*, Routledge, New York and London.

Turner, B. (1994) *Orientalism, Postmodernism and Globalism*, Routledge, London and New York.

Voll, J.O. (1991) 'Fundamentalism in the Sunni Arab World: Egypt and the Sudan', in M.E. Marty, and R. Scott Appleby (eds), *Fundamentalisms and the State*, University of Chicago Press, Chicago.

Walby, S. (1990) *Theorizing Patriarchy*, Blackwell, Oxford and Cambridge, MA.

Wali, S. (1995) 'Muslim Refugee, Returnee, and Displaced Women: Challenges and Dilemmas', in M. Afkhami (ed.), *Faith and Freedom: Women's Human Rights in The Muslim World*, Syracuse University Press, Syracuse, NY.

Williams, R. (1973), 'Base and Superstructure in Marxist Cultural Theory', *New Left Review*, No. 82 (November–December).

Yamani, M. (1996) 'Some Observations on Women in Saudi Arabia', in M. Yamani (ed.), *Feminism and Islam: Legal and Literary Perspectives*, New York University Press, New York.

Yuval-Davis, N. (1992) 'Jewish Fundamentalism and Women's Empowerment', in G. Sahgal and N. Yuval-Davis (eds), *Refusing Holy Orders: Women and Fundamentalism in Britain*, Virago, London.

# Index

*chador*, wearing of, 45, 98
chastity, 72, 87
Chatterjee, Partha, 34
Chaudhry, M.S., 23, 27
child abuse, 109
child custody, 92, 104, 105, 106, 107,
    108; denial of, 94
children: guardianship of, 104 (rights
    of fathers, 108–9; rights of
    mothers, 109); killing of, 109
Chirac, Jacques, 3
Christianity, 15, 25, 32, 44, 57; sexual
    relations in, 21
class, social, 78–97
clitoridectomy, debate in France, 60
Colla, E., 45
colonialism, 35, 38, 51, 58; relation to
    Islamic gender practices, 86; role
    of, 17
Commins, David, 68
Competition for Citation of the Qur'an
    (Iran), 103
Congress of Eastern Women, 130
Coulson, N.J., 25
criminal responsibility, age of, 109
Cromer, Lord, condemnation of Islam,
    16

Dastghaib, Ayatollah, 103
de-Islamization, 134
death penalty, 44; abolition of, in Iran,
    57; restoration of, in Iran, 58 *see also*
    stoning to death
democracy, 10, 51, 54, 61, 63, 69, 76,
    91, 92, 96, 118, 126, 132, 133, 136,
    144, 146; rejection of, 70, 71; space
    of, 144
desecularization, 101
difference, 5, 51, 64, 96, 125, 140;
    cultural, 65, 99 (politics of, 49–63)
al-Din, Nazira Zin, 45
divorce, 20, 21, 25, 82, 92, 105, 106,
    107, 108; enforced, 45; law on,
    104; women's rights in, 19, 73
Dragadze, T., 18
dress, Islamic, 29, 41, 43, 44, 92

Eagleton, Terry, 51, 135, 141
Ebadi, Shirin, 119
Ebert, T.L., 51
Ebrahim, Fatima, 95

Ebtekar, Masoumeh, 98
education: discrimination against
    women, 94, 98, 100–1; elementary,
    compulsory, 130; of women, 116,
    117, 128; restructuring of
    curriculum, 103
Egypt, 35, 36, 67, 68, 88, 127, 129;
    charge of apostasy in, 44–5;
    feminism in, 129; veiling in, 44;
    women's movement in, 91
Egyptian Feminist Union (EFU), 129
Ehrenreich, B., 80
Eisenstadt, S.N., 69
emancipation of women, 9, 61
employment, discrimination against
    women, 94, 98
employment of women, 101, 104; as
    terrain of contestation, 111–17; in
    Iran (claimed increase in, 111–15;
    in coercive apparatus, 115; in public
    sector, 114)
Enayat, Hamid, 34
Engels, Friedrich, 79, 80
Enlightenment, 53, 61, 70, 78, 79;
    critique of, 52, 56; fragility of
    progress, 55
equal pay for women, 130
equality, gender-based, 140, 141, 142
Eribon, Didier, 59
ethnicity, 51
Ettehadieh, M., 128
Eurocentrism, 50, 53, 79; in
    representation of women, 38
Expediency Council (Iran), 106
extramarital sex, 28

al-Faisal, Toujan, 45
Fakhro, M., 40
family code, in Turkey, 127
family honour, defence of, 110
family law, in Iran, 100, 104, 105, 106,
    107
Farsoun, S.K., 32
al-Fawwaz, Zainab, 129
Fayyazbakhsh, Nafiseh, 103
female genital mutilation, 83
feminism, 8, 9, 32–48, 50, 55, 66, 78,
    82, 86, 90, 118, 120, 125; colonial,
    16; definitions of, 139–40; Islamic,
    9–10, 65, 66, 75, 106, 107,
    125–48, 135, 136, 137, 145, 146 (as

metanarratives, rejection of, 50, 51
Milani, Farzaneh, 128
modernity, 39, 78–97, 135; crisis of,
    47; critique of, 58; differentiated
    from modernization, 53, 54, 83–4;
    in Iran, 59, 87, 89, 100, 117, 121;
    paradoxical for women, 78;
    rejection of, 53, 70; rethinking of,
    53–63
Moghadam, Valentine, and issue of
    women's employment, 111–15
Mohamed, Prophet, 21, 22
money, women's control of, 41
Montesquieu, Charles-Louis de, Lettres
    Persianes, 15
Moore, Barrington, 59
moral guards, 28, 43
Morality Police (Iran), 102, 115
Motahhari, Ayatollah, 26–7
Mouffe, Chantal, 142
Movement pour la Défense des Droits
    de la Femme Noire, 60
Muhammad Shah, 57–8
mujahedin (Afghanistan) see Islamic
    mujahedin
Mujahedin-e Khalgh (Iran), 66
multiculturalism, 4
Mumtaz, K., 29
Munson, Henry, 49
murder of women, 3, 46, 82, 101,
    106, 110; unpunished, 110
Muslim Brothers, 67, 68
'Muslim Woman', creation of new,
    38–42
Muslim women, 101, 138–9, 146
mut'a see marriage, temporary

Nabarawi, Saiza, 129
Al-Na'im, A., 136
Najmabadi, Afsaneh, 142–4, 145
Nasr, S.H., 69
Nateq, Homa, 88, 57, 67, 128
National Association for the Support of
    Children in Difficulties (Algeria), 3
National Islamic Front (Sudan), 67
'New World', myth of, 19
Nicholson, Linda, 51, 93
Nietzsche, Friedrich, Thus Spoke
    Zarathustra, 52–3
Nigeria, Islam in, 18
Not Without My Daughter, 36

offices, female-centred, in Iran, 103
Operation Desert Storm, 36
Orientalism, 5, 6, 7, 85, passim 32–48
    see also anti-Orientalism
Osborne, M.L., 15, 16
Ostadmalek, Fatima, 130
other, representation of, 32–3, 51
Ottoman Empire, 86

Paidar, Parvin, 106–7
Pakistan, 11, 27, 67, 69, 132, 139
Palestinian Occupied Territories, 67
Pasdaran Corps (Iran), 115
patriarchy, 38, 39, 40, 84, 132;
    interlock with capitalism, 80; neo-,
    84
Patriotic Women's League, 88
Persia, 15
pluralism, 50, 146; of morality and
    knowledge, 53, 65
polygamy, 16, 17, 23, 85, 87, 104, 108,
    130
postmodernism, 6, 64; meaning of,
    50–3
poverty, 1, 62, 95
professions: discrimination against
    women, 100–1; women's role in,
    115
prostitution, 28, 35
puberty, celebration of, Iran, 102
public sector, employment of women,
    114
public sphere, existence of, 147
purdah see seclusion of women

Qisas (Law of Retribution), 109
Qur'an, 17, 70, 130, 131, 140, 141,
    142; gender-biased misreadings of,
    130; misogynistic interpretations of,
    127; patriarchal interpretations of,
    40
Qutb, Sayyid, 68

Rabbani, Borhan-ul-Din, 2
racism, 4, 37, 49
Rafsanjani, President (Iran), 103
Rajaii, Aateghe, 103
rape, 2, 3, 25, 28, 29, 45, 46, 82;
    marital, 94; unpunished, 110
Rattansi, Ali, 51, 56
re-Islamization, 11